Reflections of a Fly Rod

Mark Usyk

This book wasn't possible only because I was able to put my thoughts and experiences into words. No, there's always people behind the scenes, whether they're actively involved or don't even realize they're having an impact on someone else's direction. The first person I need to express gratitude to is Jordan Ross of JP Ross Fly Rods. I hadn't fully embraced the idea of writing yet when JP asked me if I'd write stories for his website, I was only flirting with the idea. Once he asked and I agreed to give it a shot, that's when the reels in my head really started peeling line. He also supported me more than almost anyone else, save for my own family. Which leads me to the second part of this dedication.

To my wife Holly for proof reading everything more than once, and for listening to me ask day after day if she was going to read more that night. I'm ever grateful for not only your work and support, but your love. And to Jacob and Carter. For reading a story now and then, for looking over my shoulder as I write often and correcting the obvious mistakes (Jacob just corrected a typo as I write this), and for giving me a reason to write. You may not realize it at this age, but as you get older you'll understand what the love and support of your family can do for one's heart. I'll never be able to thank my family enough.

Not until we are lost do we begin to understand ourselves.
-Henry David Thoreau

Table of Contents

Introduction

I don't know which I'd consider worse, catching small fish, or getting skunked all together. I guess the worse would be going to work. Unless work of course ended up becoming writing. Writing fishing stories. But writing fishing stories doesn't feel like work, so the old cliché *if you love what you do you'll never work a day in your* life becomes true, which brings me back to the original question of what I would consider worse, catching small fish or nothing at all.

They all make for good stories sooner or later, so I'd have to say that using the word *worse* doesn't seem to fit anywhere at all in the same sentence for me. Worse relates to something that could be wrong, and when it comes to fishing, short of drowning nothing could be wrong. And there's that chance to be right even in drowning, while fishing anyways, because of another cliché thing people refer to all the time, dying doing something you love.

Writing isn't what I do for a living, but then again neither is fishing. I'm just your typical everyday Joe getting through life one day at a time, one job at a time, one fish at a time or more often one fishless day at a time, one story at a time. But these days fly fishing and writing are the only things that make me feel alive, so I guess perhaps they aren't what I do for a living, but just what I do to live.

I started fly fishing because I was getting bored with a spinning rod in my hand, and to tell the truth, there was something romantic at the time about the mystery of fly fishing to me, the images of loops in the air and the arch of a slim nine foot rod of graphite or glass or even bamboo. At the same time I'd always thought of writing being somewhat of a romantic thing. I was a fabricator for many years and my shop was filled with quite a few old tools, one of my favorites being an old cast iron drill press from the 1930's that still ran on straps rather than rubber V belts. A friend had once told me that there were plenty of new tools that could replace my old and weathered machines, but that I was too much of a romantic to switch to new, streamlined and more efficient equipment. I laughed at him at the time but now I can see what he meant, and that maybe he did know what he was talking about after all.

Telling stories is possibly the oldest tradition the human race has ever had. Even before a spoken language, there were always cave drawings of animals, of human figures in pursuit of them, and grunts and nods of approval in the background while bushy eyebrows raised in excitement as a story teller scratched out the scene, reliving the story and putting it up there for future generations to marvel at. Stories have always been important to us, and always will be. However it's a well-known fact that fisherman have always had the best stories. Why? Because all fisherman are liars, and liars tell the grandest stories of course.

The bulk of the stories in this book were at one time new stories up on my weekly blog on my good friend Jordan's website, JPRossflyrods.com. One hand shake deal between friends, and before I knew it I had over fifty short fly fishing stories and counting up on his site. People I worked with, some of my wife's friends even, began reading them. And then some people I didn't know. Some of them didn't even fish which started me thinking. Just like I tell people when I go out the door with a fly rod in my hand that it's not always about the fish, if people who didn't fish read my stories, maybe the stories aren't always about fishing exactly. What finally hit home for me, the thing that pushed me over the proverbial edge to put them and some other new stories into book form was when my buddy Dale at work told me that he liked my stories because they were just the right length for when he sat on the toilet in the morning. You just can't argue with tried and proven logic like that.

So I began compiling stories from the blog and the various notebooks and scraps of papers and this is the finished product. I fought the idea of calling myself a writer for quite a while, as if admitting to it or accepting the title would somehow turn it all on end and ruin it. But here I am, writing the introduction to my first book, with two other books both approaching the half way point. Who knows where it all leads. A story is really never over is it? There's always more to tell, editing, revisions, or even sequels. Jordan asked me as we walked out on our last brook trout trip of the year where I saw myself in three years with this whole writing thing. I thought for a few seconds and then gave him my answer. *Fishing.*

Reflections of a Fly Rod

It's only nine feet of graphite and a handful of cork. It's such a simple thing, not a complicated device by any means. Practically a stick in the simplest of descriptions. Yet to really immerse myself into the backstory of how this all came about, of what it does for my mind, of the things I feel when I stand at the water, of the things I *don't feel* because I stand at the water, it stirs up more questions and answers that lead to still more questions and answers. So I may start to see that if there's really no meaning to life, if by some chance we weren't each put on this planet to do something specific, then the odds of falling into something that feels like just that, that it's what you're meant to do, they must be so small and remote in such a vast time and place that it seems proof enough that there must be a master plan for my life somewhere. The meaning of life is in my grasp. Literally at my fingertips.

Just like an old friend, this rod's traveled many a back road with me as I worked far from home for a living, as well as specifically setting off in search of the wild trout that call the Adirondacks their home. The rod may weigh no more than ounces, but the water and dirt that have clung to it, the fish slime that's dried on the handle, and the memories attached to it all add up to what would be a great weight if it was a sad thing. But instead, each time I feel its lack of heft, its perfect balance and the smooth cork in my grip, a great weight is lifted. Just like an old friend, its company is always welcome, and the reminiscing begins simply at its sight or even mere mention in conversations. We've been through a lot together in a short time, this rod and me, and none of it short of great days and wonderful stories. Fish or fishless, the stories are more proof that perhaps we *are* meant to do something specific after all.

It's got some scratches, it has scars. Each one like a sentence in a story helping to tell the great tale. But this one is my tale. Everyone has their own tale to tell, but the cover of my book looks different from all the other books on the shelf, because this rod wasn't built to be set on a store shelf and plucked from a line that all look identical, no this rod was built specifically for me. Like that old engraved shot gun that's been handed down through the family, the one the next generation waits excitedly to receive, this rod will be a family heirloom should my sons wish to have it.

Brookies in remote streams, browns and smallies from the most beautiful hidden stretch of the Saranac River, bass out of retention ponds surrounded by looping highway exit ramps, and perch and other pan fish while waiting for helicopter rides to mountain tops. This rod has seen some of the most beautiful places there are to see in New York State, and been with me exploring quite a few urban waters as well. Waters ignored by locals who wouldn't think twice to fish such littered and lousy streams and ponds.

A rod built just for me. When it's all said and done, it's just a fishing rod to some. To those of us who understand, it's a way out. Or quite possibly... A way *in*.

Farther Up the Saranac

I'm at about the two-hundred foot mark, maybe a little more, on a communications tower atop Lyon Mountain in the northern Adirondacks. The day started out easy enough, exploring a small mountain stream while waiting for our ride. There weren't any fish in it but getting paid to explore a potential fishing spot while you wait for a helicopter isn't a bad deal. Then our ride approached from the east, the reverberations of props carrying from miles away filled the sky, and the exploring was brought to an end.

Most of the day has been spent flying equipment, tools, and materials up the mountain via cargo net and helicopter. It's much colder up here than I'd anticipated. I'm dressed for a hot August, but up here in the wind on the steel it feels more like October. I fight not to shiver. My foreman calls on the radio for me to finish up for the day. The helicopter is on its way up to get us. They'll make two trips taking empty crates and old equipment down before the final trip I need to be on. So get moving he says.

I hear the reverberations of the blades once again and scan the sky where the evergreen tops stab upwards into clear blue nothing. The helicopter rises and banks as it comes into view around the mountain for its only clear approach to the 20'x20' sun bleached gray, weathered and rotting plywood landing pad. My work ceases, I'm transfixed on the approach as it unfolds below me. It's not just unusual to look down on a helicopter as it lands, in this instance my nerves get a work out. After a couple years of doing this job, these heights, thin steel under my boots, wind in my face, reaching out to grab antennas on ropes with nothing but hundreds of feet of nothing between you and the ground, most days just feel like any other day walking around on the ground at this point. Except for this moment today. This is different.

My view all day has been of Lake Champlain, of the Green Mountains in Vermont, of unknown lakes and rivers and mountains across the sprawling landscape far below. I've imagined myself casting a fly on all the water I can see and exploring the small streams I know are hidden in the forests. The truth of the appeal of this job is as much in the challenge and moments of adrenaline as it is in the views. Most weeks I find myself distracted from the work at hand by simply taking it all in. Now instead of calm a certain amount of dread fills me as I watch the rotor blades pass by a support guy-wire merely feet away, these wires being the only thing keeping this tower standing, while I'm on it no less. Then as it sets down on the wooden pad only sixty some feet away from the tower its blades spin precariously close to a rock outcropping only three feet away. Disaster is a wind gust or miscalculation or an itch in the pilots nose away at any second... And I've got no place to go but down.

When the work day is done and I find myself hours later stringing up my fly rod, the view of the helicopter is still in the front of my mind. I can still feel the hot prop wash and smell of aviation fuel as it was blown upward at me, an experience I imagine very few people have had simply because most people are never *above* a flying helicopter. I choose a fly from the box, a golden stonefly with black rubber legs, and tie it on. As the scene plays out over and over in my head I still feel the stress of the situation. It takes me four attempts to tie my knot, and as I enter the river I'm hurried and clumsy. This job has changed me over the past four years. I'm not the same person I was before the climbing. In some ways I'm a better person, in others worse. It depends on who you ask.

I strip line off the reel and it coils and floats in the water next to me. I pick my intended target. A large pocket of calm water downstream of a huge boulder, and I make my cast. The line loops beautifully and rolls over, the fly landing gently on the water. The helicopter is finally gone. The stress vanishes with a cast. The Saranac River and my 3wt will be my therapist this week.

There's nothing quite like the line pulling tight and the jerk of the rod tip on your very first cast. I immediately laugh out loud. I've forgotten the day with one cast. The line darts left and right but I can feel the fish is small. It doesn't matter in the least. It's a fish, and I've caught it. It ends up being a rock bass about the size of my hand, a mix of bronze and black, with the typical large red eyes. They eat everything, little pigs with gills I call them. I return it to the water, and within two casts I've got another.

Off to my right is the hydroelectric building we parked the truck next to, the rumble of the water discharging back into the river almost drowns out the voice of my climbing and fishing cohort for the week. Mike yells to me something undiscernible, but I know it means he has a fish. He's pulled two small bass from the eddy where the river flows into the crushing discharge with his spinning rod. Nothing very big, but fish are fish when we're out like this. I suggest we get away from here, we need to make our way upstream and explore a bit. Off we go.

Our path to travel up river is unique to say the least. Where the hydro station stands there are hints that something stood here long before it was built. An old cobblestone wall stands parallel to the river. Smooth round stones outlined in rough and degrading mortar, weeds and climbing vines hide some of it, while here and there small trees grow on its top or even out of the missing mortar gaps. If there's one thing I've learned about life along my short journey, it's where there's a will there's a way.

Instead of jumping from rock to rock, I find myself stepping across huge, round, flat sided mill stones. A clue to some earlier Adirondack history, probably a pulp mill, they give us an easy start to our upstream travels, until I step on one that's submerged under a few inches of water. It's like walking on ice, and I make some clumsy but impressive maneuver as I go skating off the flat stone like a skateboarder trying a new trick for the first time, somehow landing on my feet. In water up to my waist of course. I look back to see Mike laughing. "I meant to do that, I was getting hot, the water's cool." We both laugh now, we both know I fell in. I fall in a lot. All the time.

Around a bend the rumble from the power plant discharge is now all but gone. The mill stones are gone. We find ourselves stepping from rock to rock, and I finally leave the rocks and just walk through the small pools on our side of the river. It's maybe thirty feet across here, but pretty shallow for most of it. The side we stand on is jagged broken up rock, the corners and edges only dulled by the erosion and weathering of the north country. Clumps of tall grass grow here and there mixed in with the water and rock.

14

The bulk of the river in front of us looks to be perhaps three feet deep or less, but crystal clear, every feature of the bottom visible. Crevices, rocks scattered everywhere and what looks to be an underwater ledge half buried in a rock slide from the steep outcropping flanking it. Mike goes another forty yards or so upstream. I stay here. I look out at the painting in front of me, I wish I could take it home.

I pull line from the reel and it lays on itself at my feet, half in the water and half on top the rocks I stand on. I make a cast upstream and to the far side, the loop of the line flowing effortlessly over the river as it unrolls and the wet fly lands. I strip twice to pull it away from the rocky edge and into the current running the narrow channel, the deepest water. A dark shape lets loose an ambush, and a take. This time I don't laugh, but I know I'm smiling. The rod dances, the line races cutting the water like a knife. A roll and bend of a fish shape and the jump. The hook stays and I strip line in bringing the fish closer.

The fish pulls hard and takes line off the tiny small stream reel, it's heading for some jagged rocks downstream where the water gets skinny and the current turns to rolling and foam. I'm afraid of a break off on my 6x tippet by either the rocks it's about to reach or just merely pulling back too hard, but I want to avoid the rocks more. In the end I have the fish in hand. A smallmouth something unlike another I've never seen. Dark, perfect for waiting in ambush in dark shadows, the bronze almost bordering on becoming a dark orange, with warrior like vertical markings, the stripes making me think of a huge cat waiting for its prey in the tall grasses of India. Earlier I'd caught a pig with gills, now I had a tiger with scales. I took a couple pictures and released Shere Khan back to hunt once more.

We fish this stretch for the next hour and move up a little farther, until we decide as the sun is dropping into the trees that we'd better pick our way back while we can still see. Tomorrow after working on the mountain we'll return again and go farther. We've got four days. Four days to keep going farther, to find what's around the next bend.

The next morning as we unloaded the John Deer side-by-side from a trailer at the base of Lyon Mt, Mike and I discussed the great section of

15

river we'd found the day before. We wanted to get through the work day as fast as we could so we could get back to the Saranac and find out what was around the next bend, and the next after that. There was no helicopter getting us to the top today. It had showed up to carry big heavy crates of expensive microwave dishes and equipment safely to the top, and now that all we had to get to the top was us, it was gone and we were left unloading a four wheel drive side-by-side that had *no* business climbing what hardly passed for a mountain path.

For the rest of the week it would be up to us, a four man crew clawing its way up the mountain on a two man ATV. Two front seats and a small bed. For something that had no business going up there, business was good. What could possibly go wrong in the middle of nowhere anyways?

As we started up the goat path, left behind by the installation of the power poles that carried electricity to the tower site at the top, Mike and I sat on top of our climbing harnesses in the tiny utility bed and I read the warning sticker next to my feet where they braced me against the front. "Warning. No passengers in bed. May result in serious injury or death." I pointed to it and we both laughed. Then we hit the first washout full of boulders and the ATV jolted and pointed skyward as it tilted sideways. What was a couple minute trip to the top by helicopter ended up being an hour and a half trip one way by ATV. This week the challenge wasn't just working on a remote communications tower on an Adirondack mountain top, it was getting there, and getting back. And not dead or maimed would be nice too.

Three hours of clawing up and down a "path" that would've had rock crawling Jeep guys envious made our day even longer. After working up there all day, even taking in the beautiful views of the Adirondacks and the Green Mountains of Vermont to our east didn't take away from the fact that when the day was done at 3:30, we still had an hour and a half of white knuckle sliding, tipping, jolting, bumping, and scraping back down the mountain before we could begin our half hour truck ride back to the Saranac River to end our day the right way.

When we finally pulled the truck up next to the power station and the rumbling of the water discharging back into the river again we were in a hurried state of stringing up rods and changing into shorts as fast as we could. We cast to the waters we'd already fished only as we passed by them. A walleye from the shallow waters just above the hydroelectric building discharge was my first unexpected surprise. It was only about thirteen inches, but the last thing I expected to find on the end of my fly rod. Apparently walleye can be taken on the fly rod with a black Woolly Bugger. And why not? It's a fish. It eats stuff that looks alive. You learn something every day.

We passed by the water I'd caught the tiger striped smallmouth from the day before, and on our way through Mike caught a small brown about nine inches and I caught another smallmouth of about the same size. Nothing to write home about, but nothing to complain about either. We weren't working after all. We kept going, moving at a hurried pace upstream. We'd lost an hour and a half off our fishing time by the ATV ride down and we meant to make some of that up.

As we passed the last place we fished the day before we rounded a bend we hadn't reached previously and I think we both felt like we'd just hit the lottery. There was no easier going from this point. There was no more stepping from rock to rock, no more walking through a foot of water to get where you wanted to go. The sides of the river were now huge boulders, ledges, and rock faces. To get to the other side where the travel looked easier would mean a possible swim. The river narrowed here substantially, but where it lost width it gained depth and speed. After handing fishing rods back and forth as we took turns climbing a few large rock outcroppings that time had beaten and Mother Nature had cast down onto the river's edge, we found ourselves looking down on the river from about eight feet up.

Below us we had a bird's eye view of a small pool surrounded by boulders. The water came fast from above it, crashing past rocks that had refused to be moved, only shaped over time by the power of the water, and above this stretch there was a huge pool at the bottom of a good sized waterfall. Now the game was set. The question was to cast to this pool that most definitely held a couple fish, or to pass it and make a run for the giant pool below the waterfalls? I looked at Mike,

17

he was eyeing the waterfalls too. But it was early enough. I removed the black Woolly Bugger from the hook keeper on my 3wt again and stripped line. Mike readied a small soft plastic minnow on his spinning rod. I made the first cast.

A fish shape shot out from under a deep boulder as I stripped the bugger past it, making it jerk and twitch in the current. A quick tug and the fish was gone. As I stripped the line back in Mike made his first cast, the rubber minnow lure taking almost the same route as my bugger. The same fish shot out once again and this time it was caught. A standard looking, probably stocked brown about eight or nine inches once more.

I moved up to some water not so fast just below the pool where the water sped up some but hadn't narrowed and picked up white water speed yet. I cast to some churning water coming off some rocks just below the surface and as it washed out of the turbulence and into the calm the line pulled hard and the rod bent. "Yeah!" The fish fought towards stronger current once it realized something wasn't quite right. It's something programmed into every smallmouth it seems. The rod stayed bent for the better part of five minutes as I cautiously kept tension but tried to meter my enthusiasm as to not break off the light tippet and loose the fish.

There's something about that short 6' 6" 3wt that my good friend JP built me years ago, that just makes about any fish on the line, no matter how big or small, seem to be one of the greatest stories ever to me, before I even catch a glimpse of the fish. The rod was bent, the line tight and it sliced through the water like the cliché knife through butter. The jump and the thrash of the fish above the crystal clear Adirondack current made my heart pound in my chest. Another great, dark colored smallmouth. At the same time I was working on bringing the bass in, Mike caught yet another small brown.

We decided this was most likely the greatest stretch of river we'd found while working on the road to this point. It had to be. We'd done a lot of fishing together and had our favorite towns with favorite waters scattered across the state, but this one was something more special. Not because of the quality or size of the fish, but because of the setting.

18

The fact that we were no more than a mile perhaps from our parking spot, and we'd run out of beaten path early on was great. The landscape was one National Geographic quality photo opportunity after another, and there was no trace of people. No beer cans. No fishing line tangled in the trees. Not even a foot print. And we found fish. We spent a couple hours fishing below the giant pool before making our way back downstream to the truck just before dark. The pool and the falls would be tomorrow's mission.

The third day found Mike and I up on the tower in the bright sun under beautiful blue Adirondack skies, wearing rain jackets, wishing we'd had ski jackets and face masks. The rain jackets were a feeble attempt to break the wind and hold in what little body heat we had left, the sun and blue sky were a cruel joke which started when we parked the trucks and saw what the morning news told us we'd see...sun and no clouds. The punch line came when we climbed the tower and harnessed off, leaning back and looking out over the sprawling green that spread in every direction to the horizon.

As we waited for our tools and materials to make their way up to us on the rope, we began to realize that although the day appeared to be a warm late summer day down on the ground, it was much cooler, even more so today than in the previous two days, up here on the tower. The longer we shivered the more we began to question whether we'd actually want to go walk a river in shorts and get our feet wet. But reaching the bottom of the mountain path once more at the end of the day there was no question. It was warmer down here. Down here we'd be sweating in those rain jackets. We pointed the truck to the Saranac River.

Just like the second day, we made casts to all the places we'd lingered and fished the days before, only moving upstream faster, with a purpose. We were on a mission to fish the huge pool at the base of the waterfall. Small browns, fall fish, and smallmouths greeted us at the ends of our lines as we made our way. On our third day I felt as if we knew this short stretch as we knew old friends.

Finally we stood on jagged and uneven boulders, protruding from the river at uncomfortable and extremely steep angles as they did their best to stop the tail waters of the pool while it flowed around them and downstream. As we took in the picture perfect scene we did our best to stand on slippery and steep rock that wanted nothing more than to send us off flailing in the current. We studied our surroundings, thinking that to move around and fish the pool we'd have to cross to the other side by jumping large gaps of open water with small landing zones of pointy, wet rocks. I tried to make the first jump several times, my mind was willing, but my feet refused to let go of the rock they stood on. White water blasted by. We looked around a little more.

I don't know which one of us found it first, but the most amazing path cut out of the shear rock ledge led us above and around the pool on the left side. Climbing some collapsed rock face we followed a path on the ledge which was in turn covered overhead by yet another shear rock face. I could picture myself camped here, a small fire burning, the heat reflecting off the stone and the fire reflecting on the water. Like something out of a movie, it seemed almost to perfect.

We fished from the ledge for quite a while, catching a couple small trout and bass, but we needed to go farther. It looked as though we could carefully hike and climb our way up the side of the waterfall feeding the pool, and we both agreed, we needed to know what was up above the falls. It was painful leaving the ledge and the pool, but new excitement filled me as we ascended the left side of the falls, slowly making our way up wet and slippery flat rock with white water only feet away waiting to pummel us off stone and wash us into the pool below.

Above the falls was white water. Above the white water was another smaller pool with a strong eddy separating the shallow far side from the deep water in the middle. Here I let my fly line drift and a bugger do its thing. Smallmouth in the eight to ten inch range were more than happy to attack and after fishing out this pool we moved up stream once again. After handing rods back and forth and some fairly hairy rock climbing with nothing but water below us we found the final pool on our short excursion. One below an extremely tall dam. Here the Smallmouth were no bigger, possibly even smaller, but seemed more vicious. How many times I laughed at the jump and thrash to find a bass that would fit in the palm of my hand I don't know, but I'd forgotten the hard week on the tower. Life was good once again.

Such a beautiful stretch of river. Such a secluded stretch of diverse runs no more than an enjoyable hike from a parking spot next to a noisy power station. Being so close to the road and to an obvious fishing spot at a parking area you'd think it would be fished out, littered with drink bottles and tangled fishing line. But it wasn't. The fact is, we would've never found any of it if we weren't willing to go farther than everyone else. Sandwiched between a power station and its dam upriver which fed it was the most amazing landscape we ever fished while working and fishing on the road in four years. It took wading, hiking, rock hopping, and some rock climbing to find it, and it was ours for two weeks. We never saw another person, never another vehicle parked.

Later in the first week Mike ended up catching a really nice brown from the pool below the falls that was around eighteen inches give or take. So we'll call it twenty. I caught another great smallmouth from the same place. I often think back to that pool and picture myself standing on a flat rock table at the immediate bottom of the falls. A place that wasn't reachable until the water levels dropped during the following week. I see myself standing there with water crashing down to my left and pouring off a flat ledge to my right, and my fly line looping overhead. It lands in the white water and the current carries the stonefly to the tail out, and I strip it back, casting again. Perfect cast after perfect cast, in a perfect place.

Firsts

Firsts. Firsts are something special. First steps. First words. First day of school. First love. First kiss. First job. First car. First house. First baby. Firsts are something you normally don't forget. And even if you do, it only takes the slightest of hints in any normal day's event to bring the memories back to you from out of nowhere. Firsts are always of some importance. And then there's fly fishing firsts.

Your first rod and reel. Your first time trying to cast. Your first snagged tree. Your first wind knot. Your first lost fly because of a poor knot. You really thought you'd tied it right. The first trout to rise to your dry fly, and then your first miss at a rising trout. Your first thoughts that maybe you should just stick to your spinning rod.

But there's something to this fly fishing thing. You can't figure it out, but when you decide you're going to go fishing, even though you've got the spinning rod back in your hand again, your first thought is that you should be trying the fly rod a little more, that you shouldn't give up on your first attempt. You have to *learn first* before you can decide if it's for you. The first time you pick up the spinning rod after getting frustrated with the fly rod, then lay the spinning rod back down in the bed of your truck and walk back to the water with the fly rod...

Then it begins to happen. Your first fish on the fly. You stand on the edge of a small pond, cast your first little foam popper. You let it sit for ten seconds, and on your first strip, pop, and pause...Your first pan fish on the fly. And now, for the first time, it all seems much more reachable. Like the first pan fish on a worm below a bobber when you were knee high to a grasshopper, this little pan fish, like so many other pan fish you've caught through your lifetime, this one suddenly feels like your first all over again. And in a way, it is.

It only rolls on from there. Until one day, not far off, you stand in a river. Your rod flexes, loads, unloads, and loads again as you gain distance and finally let the line shoot forward through the guides. The line stretches out straight before you and seems to come to a pause and hover in midair before gently dropping, the dry fly falling and landing with hardly a disturbance to the surface. The drift is right. The placement where it needs to be, drifting directly over the rising trout you've been watching for a couple minutes. There's a subtle take, not a splash, but merely a sip from below and your fly is gone. Your first perfect cast. Your first good drift. And your *first* trout on a dry fly.

Since picking up fly fishing, every new fish caught on the fly rod, no matter how many I'd caught before on the spinning rod, it feels like a first all over again. My first fish on the fly rod was a six inch...ok, four inch fall fish. A minnow. I watched them taking little brown bugs off the surface in the creek out back one day, tied on a little brown *thing*, and finally made the good cast and caught my first fish on a dry fly. I laughed, and then I gained some confidence. I bet I caught ten of the little things that day. First pan fish on a popper. First bass on a streamer. There were countless misses at trout on dry flies, until one day it finally happened. First trout on a dry. An eight inch brookie at a spot everyone said it shouldn't have been. Five minutes later in the same spot, the first brown on a dry, a nice twelve incher that felt like a twenty incher because I hadn't yet felt a decent fish on the fly.

They're all fish I've caught before on spinning rods. But now every new species checked off on the fly rod feels like a first all over again. When we keep getting older, it's nice to discover something that can almost make you feel like you're going back again. For someone that doesn't fly fish yet, this is their second chance at a first all over again. You point out someone to me that wouldn't love the feeling of the first time all over again and I'll point someone out to you that's dead inside. There isn't a fish yet that didn't make me smile when I found it at the end of my leader, but there's a first for everything I suppose. I'm waiting on my first rubber boot. On the fly rod I bet they fight like hell.

Fishing on the Road

For *three days* we'd given it our best shot. Driving from the job site in Big Flats NY to our hotel in Elmira, I'd located what was supposed to be a *trout stream*. Looking down from the cell tower we were working on, a hundred and fifty feet up, it actually flowed by no more than two-hundred yards from where we worked, and after staring at it most of the day I'd convinced myself that my 3wt rod was not only perfect for the tiny stream, but that it would find a trout within the first three casts. On the first day, I was wrong. Mike, with his spinning rod, also found nothing at the end of his line over and over. I managed to catch two more branches than trout on the second day. Seeing as how I caught two branches, the second day was also a bust.

We also drove over to a large pond that was actually named on the maps, one we could see about a mile away from our perches up on the tower, because it was water and we could see it. So it had to have fish. It was named, and it was part of a town park, containing walking paths and foot bridges, how could it not have fish? Upon arrival we found fish everywhere. Dead, rotting carp that is. Location number two, also a bust.

I'm never angry or disheartened over getting skunked, but the job we were sent to do and the project manager that sent us to do it were both trying to break our wills and our backs. We were climbing on stuff we shouldn't have been climbing on, working with stuff we'd never worked with before, and opening up coax lines in weather we shouldn't have been opening lines in. Just one fish on each of our lines would've been nice. Just one. It seemed the waters and the fish were also working against us this time around. Come on, just one tiny, lousy fish was all we asked for.

Each day driving Highway 86 between the hotel and the job site we passed a massive retention pond crowded on all sides by pavement. The highway ran parallel on two sides, and on and off ramps flanked it on either end. We joked about pulling off and hopping the chain link fence each morning and each afternoon as we drove by it at 70mph, but on the third day after striking out in better places, the decision was made as it came into view. Twisted Sister wailed "We're Not Gonna

Take it" in my head. Or maybe it was the little red version of myself standing on my shoulder singing in my ear and dancing like a giddy school boy with horns and a pitch fork, but either way, this was happening. *Now*.

We slowed our speed enough to let close traffic pass us, and as we passed the water on our right, coming to the end of it but just before the off ramp, we slammed on the brakes and ripped the steering wheel to the right, the truck coming to a rest on the shoulder in a cloud of dust. Feeling like we shouldn't be here I backed the truck into the high brush along the end of the fence, the sound of scraping paint on thin branches making me grin like a mischievous teenager. Mike and I hopped out of the truck and to our delight there was an opening in the fence. It seemed as though we weren't the first to make this decision.

Fly fishing is full of challenges, and this may be part of its appeal for me. Matching the hatch. Reading the water. Finding the fish. Keeping my back cast above and off the 8ft chain link fence on the incline to my back and out of the small scrubby trees all around me while timing it to avoid eighteen wheelers traveling at 75mph and creating one heck of a whirl wind as they passed no more than twenty feet behind me, now that's a challenge you won't find on remote Adirondack streams or picture perfect western freestone rivers.

It wasn't a great week for fishing. We didn't come across post card views and beautiful wild trout or record shattering largemouths. But I can tell you that the first bass to bend my 6wt rod on the side of that highway as traffic blew by to our backs on the other side of the fence...that's one fish I'll never forget. The next day we stopped again, with two trucks. We finally got back to the hotel after dark. I'll never look at a retention pond on a highway the same ever again.

Hope is at the End of Every Cast

A small river I'd never been on before, over a state line far from home. Out the back door of a roach motel and through the woods, the map on my cell phone had shown me the water that you'd never know flowed through otherwise. What was its name? Not important. It was a river. A small river. My favorite. I knew by the satellite picture which way the river flowed simply by zooming in and seeing the current coming off the downstream side of the rocks, so I traveled in a direction that would put me downstream of a section that looked to have lots of large boulders. That was if I could manage to walk in a straight line through the woods.
Doubtful.

Passing under tall second growth evergreens lined in perfect rows, the carpet of rust colored needles was like walking on sponge, a couple small forests of ferns mixed in here and there broke up the well-ordered pines. Spider webs spanned from tree to tree but weren't noticed twice until I found them on my face and in my hair. It was a good day not to be a bug I thought. The trees stood at the cut out bank like soldiers standing at attention, guarding the water on both sides with honor in silence. I stepped from the high bank down to the dry coble stone river bottom, round stones bleached white from a dry summer. If it were early spring or after a good rain I was sure I'd already be knee deep in the current.

The water was clear, but moved very slowly, swirling around boulders, the pockets behind them looking to be the only place deep enough to hold fish on such a warm summer afternoon. Small little Black Gnats were hovering in swarms above the water and every now and then I'd contort my lips to one side or the other to blow one away from my mouth or swat one from my eyes. Not seeing any fish rising anywhere I tied on the old faithful black Woolly Bugger, just a buggy looking thing for all intents and purposes, and picked a pocket to cast to. The short 3wt rod, perfect for such a place, knew right where I wanted the fly to go, and cooperated, coming just short of the pine branches behind me, and still reaching the first pocket water to my front.

I expected nothing, but hoped for something. *Hope* is at the end of every cast, and nothing is better than hope. Because even if the line goes tight and you bring a fish to your hand, once that fish goes back, the hope of another is always there, prodding you to cast again and again, stacking up experiences and memories to carry with you and feed more hope.

I've never been a head hunter, just trying to catch as many fish as I possibly can at all costs. I've never targeted river monsters or lake lunkers, trying to catch the biggest fish wherever I go. Instead, I've always targeted waters I've never fished before and scenery that calms my thoughts, quiet and void of other people and other voices. I think that's why I enjoy every outing I go in search of fish... Because I'm not really searching for fish. I'm searching for hope, and searching for hope feeds the search for more hope, and hope is at the end of every cast. Whether it be a ten inch bass, an eight inch trout, a hand sized beautifully colored and marked pan fish, or even a true trophy. I guess I'm not targeting big fish. I'm targeting hope.

My wife says I'm a pessimist. She's right. I'm not a guy that views a glass as half empty or half full. I'm the guy that says a glass of piss half empty or half full is still a glass of piss. If you see me smiling too much, something's probably wrong. Except on the water. On the water, every fish, big or small, is a good thing. Every cast is a chance to hope. And *hope*, hope is at the end of every cast.

Who's the Real Sucker?

I'm in Elmira NY. A few weeks earlier I was here for work and before the week was over, after several failed attempts fishing a couple small streams and one large river, we found ourselves hiding the truck behind a guard rail and some bushes and fishing a retention pond in the middle of the highway... with success no less. Last night after checking into our hotel room, I grabbed my waders and my fishing pack and made a short walk down to Newtown Creek, a small tributary to the Chemung River that three of us were skunked on our last trip down here.

The Chemung River was right out the back windows of the hotel, and I mean that literally. We climbed out our windows to check it out. We're adults, I swear. Well, I am anyways. One of the kids that climbs with us just turned twenty-one last week, and the other guys are all at least ten years younger than me. And none of us act like adults, so it's all up for debate. If you're only as old as you feel then I'm in my mid-seventies. But if you're only as old as you act then I'm about seventeen. Just ask my wife.

Anyway, the Chemung River. It's a shallow, wide, dingy greenish, filthy looking thing, and I've never caught a single fish out of it here the several times we've worked in the area. I'd found a few sources online telling me that there was a small population of stocked browns, many being decent to large sized hold over fish in the Newtown, and after a long, hot day on a black rubber roof relocating a group of antennas, the fact that we didn't see so much as a minnow the last time we were here didn't do much to deter me this time. Wading a shady, cool creek seemed like a good plan. I found no trout.

After drifting an olive bugger through a couple slow runs and twitching it across a handful of pools I climbed my way up a steep bank to the walking path that paralleled the creek, scratching my head that I couldn't even come up with a rock bass the size of my hand or smaller, which would've at least beaten the skunk. I made my way about a hundred feet upstream and then left the path once more to look down on another slow run, standing and studying the water, looking, no, *hoping* to find clues, to just see some type of movement. Anything. A

28

freaking turtle would have made me happy at this point. Something. And then it happened.

I saw a long, dark shape at first, then it flashed a pale side and sank back into the dark creek bottom. Finally. I knew what it was too. It was a fish. I'm not a picky fisherman by any means, I'll cast a fly at anything with fins, and suckers have fins. Most everyone I know hates them. They cuss them when they're found at the end of their lines and wish nothing but to get rid of them before picture proof can be taken that would surely lower their fisherman statuses, but I'm not picky. I believe every fish has its place in the water, and just because the suckers place is on the bottom doesn't make it a *bad* fish. Many times in the creek behind my home, when the trout aren't biting, when the smallmouths are laying low and eluding me, the suckers and creek chubs and fall fish can fill in for the more desirable fish's absence.

I found as I walked farther upstream still only a few hundred yards from the mouth where it flowed into the Chemung, as I looked down on a large tail out, that in these spots of broken water, the suckers had moved in preparing to spawn. I know at the tails of these riffles that they're sitting there, just like a trout would be, waiting for their meals to be churned up off the bottom and right to them. They were still on their way upstream, not spawning yet, and I didn't know if they'd eat or not, but I had nothing to lose and a couple hours of daylight.

Looking down at tail fins and dorsal fins protruding from the rough current every few seconds, I could see them in groups of four to even six or seven, and I knew from previous experiences, that I could probably get within mere feet of them if I came up from behind them, from downstream, because just like trout, they face upstream waiting for their food to come to them in these spots. I've actually touched one on the tail with my hand before it knew I was there.

So here I stood, finally fish, fish I could even *see*, fish I could possibly grab with my bare hands, but I'd leave the noodling to the southerners and their cat fish. These fish I'd catch with my fly rod. I made my way down the steep, overgrown, slick bank, and when I was about five feet from the water's edge the mud got the best of me and I covered the last few feet very quickly...On my ass.

29

I stood up and cussed the fact that climbing towers always made me think I was better on my feet under any circumstances. It didn't bother the suckers, they were still there, resting almost motionless on the bottom under the shallow, rough riffles. Every now and then one would roll on its side over another, a pinkish-red tail and brown-gold scales. It was a small piece of water, maybe twenty feet wide, with a pool above it, the riffles originating from a wall of large rocks spanning the width of the creek. The water tumbled over the rocks just beneath the surface and continued into a pool that was probably less than three feet deep where it never really flattened out, only kept churning on the surface over the backs of the fish, motionless in the calm water beneath before it finally settled down a couple feet behind them and continued flowing downstream as another slow, deep run.

I stood downstream from them a good twenty feet and off to their left. I still had on the small olive colored bugger and decided there was no reason to change it yet, as if the first hour of catching nothing with it wasn't enough of a clue. I've got a hard head. Just ask my wife. My casts landed just above the hidden wall of rocks at the head of the section and the bugger would wash down over and into the slightly deeper water where the fish waited on the bottom. It tumbled and bumped its way over the round stones that covered the bottom as it closed the distance to the fish...and went right on by. Several times. I started going over in my head what I had in my fly box and finally gave up on the bugger after a couple dozen casts with nothing at the end of them.

I opened my fly box and looked over its offerings. Nymphs. Nymphs were probably the ticket. I chose a very tiny one, a size 20 hook, and tied it on.

My next couple dozen casts with the tiny offering also went unnoticed. I tried a slightly larger bead head nymph, with the same results. Zero. Nada. Nothing. I tried another, and another, and well, I lost track of how many I tried, but guessing now, I'd say *all of them*.

I got desperate. I tied on my last ditch effort bug that's proven to catch just about anything that swims, a size twelve hook with red marabou, the tail about the length of the hook shank. Tied with a lot of marabou, it's a streamer with enough meat to entice everything from bass to walleye and pickerel. Tied with very little material, they're carried with the current just off the bottom of a shallow stream bumping and tumbling along, perhaps imitating the simplest of all fishing baits, the worm. But let's get this one thing straight. It's not a San Juan worm. I'd never sink low enough to just tie a piece of chenille to a hook. A small pinch of red marabou however is at least feathers. So it's a fly. Right? I tied on the latter version and thought five casts. *Five casts and if nothing takes it, I quit, and I'm going back to the hotel.* A couple dozen casts later I reeled in all the fly line and made my way up the bank.

I changed out of my waders and took my work boots out of my pack. As I was squatting in the middle of the trail tying my boots, and admiring the custom 3wt leaning against a tree to my side I heard the sound once again of suckers splashing in the shallow water. I couldn't help but think to myself... Who's the real sucker?

Hudson River Smallmouths

I spent quite a bit of time fishing the Hudson River in various places throughout New York State while I worked on the road doing the cell tower gig. I've fished it where it's nothing more than a small creek in the high peaks region near Mt. Marcy and the fish you find are the wild Adirondack brook trout that average around six inches. I had the opportunity many times, while working anywhere between Gore Mt. and Lake George to fish several sections where it's a wide, rock strewn but still shallow enough for wading, full size Adirondack river of crystal clear water holding browns and smallmouths, and below the dam in Glens Falls where the river is no longer good for wading but holds much bigger fish and is a very dark, deeper, faster moving water.

Then finally I've fished it as it passes through the city of Albany, a huge, horribly polluted river. Bordered with signs warning you not to eat your catch, I caught mostly cat fish and had a huge northern pike break an old spinning rod as it shot from beneath the dock I was fishing from and smash the cat fish on the end of my line. I can tell you that it did finally free the cat fish as I was pulling in the line hand over hand and had it next to the dock, and that the poor cat fish, bleeding and most likely returning to the bottom after I released it to die, knew what it felt like to get hit by a train...with teeth.

I should add that I did look down on the river while working up on a couple towers down near NYC, but as diehard of a fisherman as I am, after seeing how disgusting the river was miles north in Albany, I just couldn't bring myself to try and brave the city traffic to attempt to find some access to the mighty Hudson where I'd find even worse polluted water and garbage littering the banks no matter where I went. I still question whether I should've just so I could say I'd fished it nearly from its beginning to its end, but it's not something I spend much time dwelling on. I've fished the better parts.

My most fond memory of the river took place in Glens Falls, about a mile below the dam, and just outside the Adirondack Park a few miles. Myself and a co-worker, one of my on the road fishing partners Matt, decided one afternoon that we should drive south from the hotel instead of north to look for a fishing spot on the Hudson. The satellite

32

map on my phone showed the dam down river, and I figured below that somewhere would be as good a place as any to try. Once we got there we found that we couldn't get anywhere near the bottom of the dam, so we began to cruise the neighborhood south of it to try to find some access to the river.

After asking a guy with a gray beard and a pony tail half way down his back with a pack of smokes rolled up in his sleeve, sitting out in front of his house, if there was a place to get to it, he pointed to the shoulder of the road. He took a drag, then nodded his head towards the woods. "Take the trail and follow it." He said it would bring us right to the river. It wasn't the greatest neighborhood, but then again it wasn't my truck either. We grabbed our fishing gear, locked up the company truck, and left it to a fate unknown as we trotted off through the woods.

At the river we found huge car sized boulders to stand on and a deep and dark current rushing past that would most likely mean two things. Number one you'd need something with a little weight to get it down to the fish in such a fast current, and number two, if you slipped and fell in you'd be clawing yourself up a bank a mile down river. No problem. We were here, this is what we had in front of us, and we were going to fish.

Matt was cleaning up in a small piece of slack water just below the boulders we were fishing from, the bass hammering his jigs on the end of the line connected to a spinning rod, about every other cast. None of them were big, but it was catching, all we really cared about on the road.

I wasn't having any luck with the small black bunny leach streamer I was using. I saw a couple fish dart up at the streamer but nothing seemed to want to eat it, and I was having a difficult time making a cast out very far with all the trees right at our backs. I was only just starting to get decent at casting the fly rod, but if I didn't have a clearing behind me, I couldn't manage a whole lot of line out in front of me yet. I could tell Matt was feeling a little guilty for hauling in so many fish over the past half hour while I was looking the old skunk in the eye, because he kept asking me if I wanted to use some of his jigs. He seemed confused

33

when I'd turn him down, telling him no thanks, I was good. Catching or not, I was finally getting to the point where I was comfortable enough with a fly rod that I was starting to feel what I feel today when I cast. Content. Peace. Happy. Even when I wasn't catching anything, even when I'd get the occasional wind knot or hang up in a bush behind me, I wasn't getting frustrated anymore. I guess you could say *"I had arrived."*

Up river about three hundred yards it looked like the water was a lot slower on our side, and that I might actually be able to wade out a little bit and get away from the trees. We trudged through mud and ferns, past a cutout rock wall with a fire pit and a bunch of plastic lawn chairs and garbage, and found the spot to be pretty much what I'd thought. I waded out about knee deep and felt satisfied that I had the room I needed, but after several casts I realized that out in the main current wasn't where I wanted to hunt for fish anyhow. I needed to stop thinking about casting, and start thinking about fishing. Downstream from me a good sixty feet in the calm water on our side was a downed tree. The first thing I did was change flies. I still don't know why I clipped off the black bunny leach and tied on a large hellgrammite pattern but I did. Then I made a cast out about forty feet, and let it swing back in and once it was above the downed tree I began to feed more line down river.

I can still see it unfold in my head like it happened yesterday. About the time it was even with the tree and about ten feet out from it I stopped feeding line, let it sit there for a minute, and then started to strip it back up to me slowly. I'd only stripped twice. The hellgrammite came to the top and made a small wake. As I stopped to get it back down deeper I saw *another* wake, this one from the tree. It shot out into the current and I knew it had the fly before I ever felt it through the line and the 6wt rod. I just knew. In my mind I saw the fish, even though I didn't know what it was yet, I saw it inhale the fly some sixty feet downstream and under the dark water.

The line went taut, I made my first strip set on a fish, the rod pointed straight at it like someone pointing a finger in challenge at an opponent, and the battle was on. I lifted the rod and as I tried to reel in line the drag slipped and the fish took it instead, heading straight out into the main current. I wasn't smart enough to think fast yet about how I might horse the fish too much and have a break off with the light tippet, so we'll chalk it up to luck that as I reared back on the rod the fish turned and came back to the slack water where we started the fight. This was the first fish for me on the fly rod that actually put up a *real fight*, and I'm sure the smile on my face showed it.

I'll never forget the bend of the rod as finally, five minutes later, I had the fish almost close enough to land and looking up at the bend of the rod and then out at the fish just beyond my reach, realizing why it was that fly fishermen carried *nets*. My immediate thought at the moment was walking in the door Friday when I got home, giving Holly a hug, and then informing her that I needed to spend more money on fishing gear. I needed a net. I'd stand there with a big smile, she'd be so impressed.

Figuring out how to stretch my rod arm up and back behind me and to reach out with my empty hand for the furious smallmouth must've looked quite comical to Matt. I also know at that point, I realized that most likely as far as game fish went in our neck of the woods, the smallmouth had just become my favorite to chase on the fly. Matt grabbed a couple great shots while it all unfolded and they're some of my favorite to this day. It wasn't the biggest smallmouth I ever caught, but it was my first real fight on a fly rod, something you never forget. The following week there was a net in the back seat of the truck when we pulled out on Monday morning.

The La Chute

The schedule on the shop wall said "Microwave dish install. NYSP. Ticonderoga". I turned and asked the question. "Who's been up there? Where do we stay and is there *water* close to the hotel?" Jerry, one of the newer guys, maybe with us for four months now piped up... "There's no place close to fish." It was in the Adirondacks. You couldn't make me believe that if you hypnotized me. My fly rod tubes were stashed in the back seat with our climbing gear and away we went, headed north, to hang off towers overlooking whatever great views awaited us, as comfortable on our perches as the birds in the trees.

Hours later as I climbed around on a small little communications sight built atop the historic Mount Defiance, I found myself taking more time looking down on Fort Ticonderoga and the mouth of the La Chute River flowing into Lake Champlain than actually working. I laughed to the other guys up here with me. "Yea, there's nowhere to fish." There was almost more water in sight than land. We all got a good laugh as the hotel was only five minutes away.

There were two twelve pound cannons up here pointing at Fort Ticonderoga far below, and I couldn't help but think about how people just can't seem to learn from history today, and it's always been like that, this very mountain being the proof that history repeats, yet we never learn from it.

The fort was built by the French, and in 1758 the British with the help of the Mohawk Indians used the slopes of this mountain as a vantage point to attack French troops and take the fort. Then as the American Revolution was fought, the fort became a patriot strong hold, important as it controlled passage on Champlain. But they never thought the British could get cannons up to the summit and so they didn't protect it, even though the fort had already fallen once before because of the vantage points given by it. And in 1776, a British general proclaimed that where goats could go, so could men. And where men could go, cannons could be pulled behind them. The patriots were forced to abandon the valuable battlement as 12lb cannon balls rained down from above. On a side note, I'll bet someone felt like an ass that day.

36

Then once more, in 1777, the patriots ascended Mount Defiance in silence, took the British troops up top by surprise, and captured the cannons and the mountain top. They left one cannon in place and attacked the fort using the British's own artillery, and hauled the second one down the mountain where they obtained the surrender of a British saw mill, and ended up taking three-hundred British prisoners and rescuing one hundred and eighteen Patriot prisoners. What does any of this have to do with fly fishing? Well, nothing. But it's great history.

Back at the hotel that afternoon it seemed I was the only one that wanted to go find a fishing spot that day. So I did. The La Chute River was a mere two minutes from the hotel. A gorgeous crystal clear with a blue hue to it, it flowed through the small town of Ticonderoga spilling over a small dam, around boulders creating pocket water, cascading down naturally made steps and small falls, before rumbling over the violent forty something foot tall falls that was the sight of the British saw mill taken by the Patriots so long ago, now the sight of a hydroelectric station. At the bottom of these falls the water flowed to a calm, deep blue as it made its way under a covered bridge and downstream eventually mixing with the water of Lake Champlain by the fort.

I couldn't help but think at the bottom of these falls was where I needed to cast my line. But the current blasting from the bottom of the fall's chaos proved to be almost too much, I needed more weight to get my bugger down deep and I didn't have it. I used the rushing white water to push it down a couple times and managed a couple bluegills as it swung out of the seams.

After a local stopped to watch me, a conversation lead to the history of the river, the paper mill that had stood in this park when he was a young child, and how most of the trout that were caught, which were not many by his telling, were in the stretch of river above the falls. I took a quick exploration walk to survey the river above, found a trout that was willing to dart out from under the churning white water below a small falls for my silly game, and then returned to the hotel about dark. I told Mike in the hotel room "You're going fishing with me tomorrow. The water is awesome. The waterfalls are awesome. I caught a trout. You're going with me tomorrow."

For the next two weeks we worked in the area. Mike and I fished it the next day. Brown trout and ten inch and smaller smallmouths were in pockets, holes, and pools along the short stretch in town stuck between a manmade dam upstream and the huge falls downstream, and the scenery was like something out of a magazine. Apparently the stretch was stocked but it meant little to us. The following week another climbing crew was working in the general area, and this being the only hotel around, they stayed there too, and Matt joined Mike and I fishing the La Chute. While they fished with spinning rods I happily threw loops with the 3wt. It was absolutely perfect for such a place. The water was pretty darn cold, but I wet waded and dealt with it.

I'd waded to the far side of a large pool in a bend of the river and Matt had just taken a picture of me holding a trout with his phone. As I released the fish Matt slid the phone back into his shirt pocket and then bent over for something. You can see where this is going. The phone did the old escape act and made the sick *plunk* sound of technology and nature clashing in ways never meant. I remember seeing Matt's eyes bug out of his head, and he excitedly hovered his face to the water the way a cat would over the opening of a fish bowl full of gold fish, and then without a second thought, he thrust his face and arms into the cold water and re-emerged with the phone. "I got it!" He looked it over quickly and intently. "It's good, it still works!" Then two seconds later as Mother Nature finally made it to the circuits and diodes and resistors and all the man-made stuff that was never meant for nature his grin turned to a frown. "Awwww, nope. It's gone." I couldn't help but yell over with my arms thrown in the air for effect, "Way to go Matt, you lost the *only* picture of my fish!" Ahhh, what good are friends if they won't bust your chops in bad times.

We fished the spot again the next day and while doing a balancing act on a downed tree limb bouncing in the current I looked down into the clear water where two logs lay on the river bottom between me and the bank under the shade of the trees. The logs rested on the bottom, parallel to each other creating a foot wide wooden under water channel of sorts and that's where I saw it. We were working our way downstream after going as far up stream as we could and Mike and Matt were behind me fishing the small step falls I'd found the first trout in the week before. Looking down I spotted a huge brown, it had to be around twenty inches or so. I froze. The water was so clear, I was right above it. It had to know I was there, I couldn't be that lucky. Without moving my body, slowly I let out a little line, and moving the rod tip ever so slightly over the target I dropped the olive bugger down between the two logs about six feet in front of the fish. It cruised right down the channel and stopped about eight inches from the bugger and studied it for a moment. I gave it a twitch, it closed the inches wide gap. I held my breath as my heart tried to beat itself out of my chest. Then it lifted off the bottom and glided over the fly and out into the river. I knew it was too good to be true.

I fished that stretch once more a month later. As short of a stretch as it was, it was a good stretch full of character. Cool, crystal clear water and beautiful surroundings, and to think, those same waters are a part of our rich history as a country. Long before any of us cast a fly on the La Chute River, Native Americans drank from it and caught dinner in fish traps and with spears. Then the French undoubtedly lowered their faces to the same flows for a drink, and you can picture Red Coats breaking up their formations in the hot summer, swatting at relentless Adirondack black flies and seeking the cool refreshing crystal clear water of the river for relief. And finally the revolutionaries, the patriots. They also felt the same comfort of such beautiful waters. Yes, history surely does repeat itself. Of this I'm sure.

Three Flies

I look out over the trees as their branches sway in an easy breeze. Below me some 200ft down is the world that everyone else knows. The constant noise of gas and diesel motors. The bickering of coworkers. The clang of steel on steel as it's hoisted on ropes. But up here, above it all, you lose yourself in the view. It's the one saving grace of a job I've come to loathe. It's a job that's separated me from my wife and children for too long now. A job that's kept me from important events with friends and family. A job that's changed my life for good and bad.

While the world moves on below, during the short times of waiting for materials and tools to make they're journey up to you, you've got time to gaze out to the horizons and take in all that's between it and you. The world looks a lot more peaceful from high above it. The trees, the rolling hills and mountains. The lakes and rivers. They all block out the chaos of the world we live in today. I feel bad that not everyone gets to take in what we tower climbers get to see on a daily basis.

I come home on a Friday afternoon, back to the real world. The world of mail stacked on a counter next to piles of school papers, and dishes in the sink. The hectic week of a five day a week single mother with two very active young boys is extremely evident. Toys, Nintendo 3DS's, Wii controllers, action figures, NERF guns, stuffed animals. They're strewn through the house like the aftermath of a hurricane. A dirty wine glass rests in the sink alongside a plastic Spiderman cereal bowl and an Incredible Hulk cup.

I wade through it all to a room I've built on the back of the house just for me. It's something totally separate from the style of the rest of the suburban home, like a fishing lodge from some far off plot of land on the bank of a river somewhere in my mind. Yet it's very much a part of the home. Cedar slab wood covers the walls like a cabin, and old fishing rods, lures, flies. They make me feel at home as much as the hurricane aftermath I've just come home to.

A large log stands upright in a corner, stripped of all its bark and covered in teeth marks its entire surface. The wedge chewed out of it about a foot from its bottom reminds me of the place I found it and dragged it from. A tall Cedar tree trunk full of hollow cavities, figured shapes, and smooth, sun bleached character stands the full height from floor to ceiling in another place in the room. A memory of a Monday morning drive to work and the screeching of truck brakes on the bridge in town when I spotted it two-hundred yards down river. I was five minutes late to work that morning and my boots were slightly damp sitting in our safety meeting.

I sit down at my fly tying bench in a corner. Made from various pieces of wood collected from several different places work has taken me, and I take a relaxed breath. The legs are Sycamore, from a downed tree at a nightmare job site in Maryland. The cross braces for the legs, beaver chewed branches scavenged from a trip for work where I fished the upper Hudson and walked out with them after catching several smallmouth bass and a couple browns. The bench top, a mix of rough cut planks and slab wood salvaged from a previous job up north and my younger brother's wood shop. A drift wood cedar stump pulled out of the Schroon River in the Adirondacks finishes off the memories the bench holds, almost all places on the road because of the job.

The entire room Is built on such memories, every piece of wood telling a piece of a story of the places I've been, the towers I've climbed, the waters I've fished, and the things I've seen. Some pleasant, some not. But they're all part of the same tale.

I place a hook in the vice and without a plan I begin to pull materials from the shelves above the bench, and soon I have something in front of me. Something to be used on the creek out back possibly over the weekend, or some far off unknown water in the coming week. Then I tie another. Three seems to be my number. The number to settle my mind from the work week. Three flies. By the third fly I no longer hear the yelling and swearing of coworkers from the work week. I don't feel the wind on my face or in my ears anymore, the sway of the towers, or the burn of rope through my fingers.

And now I can go pick up my two boys from school with a better outlook on life. My mind has slowed down finally. Tonight I'll sit at the dinner table with them and my beautiful wife. Tonight I'll share the recliner in front of the television with my five year old Incredible Hulk.

41

The weekend will most likely consist of sitting on bleachers as my nine year old steals second and third base, and probably home, and most likely an hour or so swinging a fly rod on the Oriskany Creek before it's all said and done. I don't think about nor look forward to Sunday evening, when I'll pack my bags full of clothes and gear for the coming week. The only comfort of the packing comes with the packing of the fishing gear. Two fly rods, a 6wt and a 3wt. One a gift from my father and one a gift won in a fishing tournament, and built by my good friend JP. Several fly boxes will be stowed on Sunday night, but before the last one can be packed, the work week entering back into my mind…

I sit at the bench again with no plan. I pull materials from the shelves once more. Three more ties, three more flies for the box. Before it all begins again.

Croghan

Croghan NY. This tower was supposed to be up, completely stacked, all two-hundred feet of it, by Friday. OK, a hundred and ninety-nine feet. They didn't want it to be two-hundred, because at one ninety-nine they don't need to light it. Another foot and they've got to put a red beacon on the top and run all the electrical for it. That's true but it's a joke in my mind. Whatever.

We had the sections built and staged on the ground, and we'd done all we could up to this point without a crane. Ahh the wonderful crane. We'd passed it on the road on our way up on Tuesday morning. What I mean is, we'd been on the road, and passed it in a parking lot on the side of the road, the poor, whipped behemoth of machinery hemorrhaging hydraulic fluid all over the pavement underneath it like roadkill bleeding out on the side of the road. Some guys would take that as a bad sign considering the job. My crew, we took it as a sign that we'd probably have some extra fishing time.

This whole thing was tough in my mind. We were only two hours from home, but we had a hotel so that we could use all the daylight building time we could instead of spending four hours out of our day driving. Being that close, we all wanted to be home, but we were used to the whole *you gotta do whatcha gotta do to get the job done* thing by now. We'd be home Friday night. The problems were that right next to the hotel was a restaurant that had two stocked ponds on the property that no one was allowed to fish, and that besides pulling a big ol' bass out of the back pond and a trout out of the front pond, the only thing I wanted to do more was finish this tower, stack the very last section on the top, tighten down the last bolt, throw my harness in the truck, and go home. I wanted to see this tower stack to the end, but I was running out of time.

The crane finally made It to the job site on Wednesday, but new problems had begun to show up. Like, not being able to extend the boom for one thing. We were able to put up two sections with the boom collapsed down, but then we left the crane crew on the site to chase down wires, relays, distribution blocks, and gremlins while we explored the river around the next bend in the road.

We crossed a bridge and pulled off on the right into a parking area next to the river and got out to take a look. There was a walking bridge over the river, not more than fifteen feet wide, and it was my kind of river. Mountain goat country. White water crashed around boulders in a steep downhill descent for a hundred yards or more, small pools here and there begged you to make a cast. Some of the pools were easy to get to, some took a few seconds to gather up some courage and take a leap of faith, and after the last boulders the water quieted down into a stillwater setting, flanked by thick alders on both sides.

Mike made a few casts to the obvious places and found brookies and browns sharing the same water, and we returned to the site to find the crane crew had left on a road trip that would take them all night for a part they said would have us up and running by early morning.

The next day the part didn't fix the problem, and we stood around and watched as the boom extended sometimes all the way up and then wouldn't collapse, or the opposite, it just wouldn't extend. Whatever it was, after about four hours of farting around with the damn thing it was decided that an override button could bypass whatever electrical problem it was having and so we suited up, harnesses and wrenches and 2lb hammers and spuds, climbing helmets and the understanding that what we were doing might not be the safest thing we could do, using a crane that only moved when you pushed an override button, but we were going to get it done.

I'm not sure which weighed on my mind more. The idea that the operator was bypassing some kind of safety that wasn't working anyhow while we stacked section after section higher and higher, the fact that once we got well above the trees we were looking down on the river while my fly rod was down below in the truck, or that we were trying to stack faster than normal with a crane that moved slower and less assuredly than normal because time was running out. And like I said, I really wanted this tower fully stacked, done, when we pulled out on Friday.

We fished the river again at the very end of the day in the rain. We worked under cloudy skies all day but managed to avoid getting wet, and then as soon as we began casting the rain came down. We drove back to the hotel Wednesday evening wet and tired but because we ended the day fishing it was all good. I tried to talk the bartender into letting me throw a few casts out across the bass pond out the back windows but she just smiled and shook her head no. I'd have asked the owner, but of course he wasn't around.

On Thursday it was a repeat of the day before. Stack as fast as we possibly could with a crane that moved as slow as it possibly could, climbing higher with each hour. I took in the views in between yelling and swearing at Mike and Teddy up there with me, half breaking chops, half serious. I can still remember the cool air on my cheeks while being hot and sweaty from struggling with hammering spuds through bolt holes that didn't want to line up at a hundred and sixty feet.

And then on our way to the hotel we stopped at a dam on the Beaver River and fished the small canyon like gully on the lower side. The trees were wearing bright oranges and pinks, and knowing tomorrow was Friday I was casting for all it was worth. I knew we'd get the tower done and I'd never be back again. I didn't catch a single fish that day, not that it mattered, but my casting seemed spot on. My loops lighter than the air they unrolled in, the water catching the reflections of the bright trees all around.

Then there was Teddy and Mike. Two guys who'd just about thrown punches a few times during the past four years. Two guys quite a few years younger than me. Guys I was proud to say that I'd had their backs and they had mine regardless of swearing and arguing while hanging from the steel. They just looked like two old friends hanging out on a river, laughing and talking while purple and red leaves floated by on a current. Seeing those two standing on rocks surrounded by water and looking like old friends, I figured a river does the same for most people, not just me.

On Friday we finished the tower with enough time to make it home before five. In the parking lot we unloaded gear from work trucks and loaded it into our own, and I shook their hands. We had each other's phone numbers, and we had tons of stories between us. Some exciting, some gut splittingly funny, some almost unbelievable that we were still around to tell them. They pulled out of the gravel lot as I walked inside with our crew leader Rich.

Rich was easily several inches taller than me, a big guy who'd grabbed me by the harness several times on the towers to lift me back up from places I couldn't climb to on my own, with one hand no less. I'd seen Rich a couple times, after someone up on the tower telling him that no one could break a bolt loose, put on his harness, climb to whatever height it was, take the same wrench and the same bolt, break it loose, and then hand the wrench back, everyone on the tower feeling a lot smaller at the moment. He was a presence wherever he went that people noticed, and I liked him a lot. We'd also fished together once or twice on the road. I normally felt very small next to him, but walking across the lot on that Friday I felt a little taller. Inside I hung my harness on a hook in one of the production manager's offices and shook his hand.

Rich and I walked into another office, the project leader for the tower we'd just finished thanking us for getting it done with the lousy crane and starting right in on where we'd be going Monday. Rich cut him off. "You're going to need to give me another guy for my crew Monday." I could see the confusion. "Why, three guys isn't enough?" Then Rich looked over to me and I reached out my hand for one last hand shake. "I'm done." I won't be here Monday. I just want to say thanks for everything, it's been quite the life the past four years.

On my way home I pulled off the road alongside the Oriskany Creek and made a few casts. I didn't catch a thing, not that it mattered.

Adirondack Reasoning

The hike in was more of an impatient trot really. I only had so much time today, and the drive up took an hour and a half as it was. I wished it were closer but then if it was, it would lose most of its appeal, being easier to get to. Part of the romance of this place in my mind was the distance from home, and most anything else in all reality. If you think about it, I could've gained *three hours* of fishing time by just fishing the creek at home, but the creek at home wasn't up here. I'm getting to that point in life where I'm realizing that time is fleeting, that we don't live forever, and that you've got to make the most of it. But I'm still willing to use up some of it burning fossil fuels in the search for the perfect place. In clumsy waders and with a whippy fly rod I hurried down the trail, the sound of the water coming and going as the trail passed close to the stream and then veered away again more than once. Finally the trail ended at the small set of falls, and after my first cast, my hurried state of mind slowed to a speed of *just right*.

The olive bugger tumbled in the churning white water and washed out into the current escaping from the white chaos of the falls. It wasn't a flash, but the darting of something dark and fishy as the line went tight. Black pit eyes and fins trimmed in white. If God is real, then this is what he wants me to do, because it feels so right. If it's all because of luck, then some days it's better to be lucky than good. Whatever the reasons, I'll take it.

As I travel upstream the thought enters my mind that I may have been born a couple hundred years too late. There's nothing here to suggest people. Not so much as a beer can laying on the ground, not so much as tangled fishing lines in the tree branches. I like it. And there's no cell phone reception, because there's no cell towers up here. Finally an escape.

People in general are lazy. The lack of any evidence of humans in this place proves it to me. People would rather drive to a local river or lake and fish no more than twenty feet from the car, only to leave their trash behind where they stood because it's too much to carry it back to the car again. If I try to reason it out, it only makes me angrier.

They come in with full beers, full worm buckets, and lures still in packaging from the store. What I find is empty cans, empty plastic worm buckets, and empty lure packages. They're all ninety-nine percent lighter than when they carried it to the water in the first place because they're now *empty*, yet they can't find the strength to carry it back where they came from.

This far out, I like to think I've gone farther than anyone else, telling myself that's why I don't find trash. Truth is, I haven't found an unknown stream, it's just that most anyone willing to put in the time to come this far for a fish that's considered a trophy at eleven inches knows better than to foul up the very thing that brings them this far in the first place. Out here, I realize that I'm *glad* most people are lazy. It leaves places like this for me to enjoy on my own in peace.

Out here. Up here. The Adirondacks. The trees. The rocks. The mountains. The streams, rivers, lakes and ponds. The wild brook trout waits for me. My 3wt like the divining rod my grandfather used to dig wells, only slightly less accurate at pointing out the locations of the fish than his was at finding water. How can I be so disconnected from everything so far away out here, up here, yet be so connected at the same time? We all have the answer to the meaning of life in us, we just haven't learned to read it yet. I'm learning. At forty years old and counting...I'm learning.

Red Woolly Buggers

I'd struggled through my first year with a fly rod in my hand in spectacular failure for the most part. The casting came fairly easy when I decided to give it a try. It was the catching that challenged me. My first fish came a couple months into the struggle, if you can call a four inch minnow a fish. I've found them in the Field Guide to North American Fishes, Whales and Dolphins... So as far as I'm concerned when I catch a minnow I've caught a fish. To argue the contrary is like standing around at a wedding reception debating whether or not the little cocktail wienies can in fact be referred to as small hot dogs or not. In the end, they both make a turd. Just like in the end I'll hook minnows from time to time the same as bass or any other fish. And now that I think about it, when I do catch minnows, I sometimes refer to them as little turds. Ahhh, the universe is a mysterious place.

When I set the goal that first winter of catching a trout on the fly rod while the banks were covered in snow, I may have been a little premature in my aspirations, but I meet challenges with indifferent ignorance head on sometimes on a daily basis, so why should a winter trout be any different. My first winter I got a lot of casting practice in. I cleared a lot of ice out of the guides, and did my best on a couple of days of single digit temperatures to keep my spirits high while my fingers lost their ability to feel the fly line let alone tie a knot in a leader. I literally caught nothing but a cold that first winter. Well, probably more like three or four colds.

During my second year of the fly rod I gained some confidence. I caught my first trout on the fly, a few nice bass, and in general cut down somewhat on lost flies in trees and bushes. I was still horrible. I still carried a spinning rod with me for those times when I couldn't take the frustrations of that long, whippy, source of four letter words and just wanted to catch a fish. But as a whole I'd progressed more than gone backwards. And me being a quitter, the fact that I was still pushing forward meant something deep down inside. I was going to continue to improve, or die a horrible fly fisherman. But either way I was going to die a *fly fisherman*. Good or bad.

So that second winter as I sat at my vice thinking about the creek out back and how I was about to again take back up the struggle the following day, I shuffled through a small assortment of feathers in small bags like one would a deck of cards, in search of *what* I wasn't sure. I wasn't overwhelmed yet by mountains of hooks and materials of every sort, I was only in the beginning stages of fly tying, still convinced I was doing it to save money. My hands came to hold a bag of red marabou and I shuffled through a handful of hackle packages, coming to rest at the matching red. I then proceeded to tie up a red Woolly Bugger. A red Woolly Bugger? Yes. Why? I told you... Because the universe is a mysterious place.

The next day around noon, feeling the temperature was just about at the day's peak I layered up and fought my way into my waders. I marched down my street, a dog barking inside through a picture window alerting its owners to the fact that the crazy fishing guy is at it again. Doesn't he know it's *winter*? At the creek I found myself standing uneasily on a six foot shelf of ice, the winter hard at work trying to close off my opportunities for what could be the rest of the season. Time was limited. Perhaps a day, perhaps only hours, but soon the water would be hard all the way across. Rather than stand on the ice above the water I slid myself carefully down into the water and found it waist deep. I stripped line from the reel and made my first cast forty-five degrees upstream and across.

I made half a dozen casts, letting my strange red creation drift and drag across the bottom of the slow moving stretch of creek. Each one came up empty. I wondered to myself why I'd tied such an odd fly, why I hadn't just gone with a typical olive or black, or why I didn't just fish a tiny nymph like everyone else would this time of year. Then I remembered my head-on ignorance. Ah yes. I wasn't doing anything out of the ordinary after all. I cleaned ice from the guides for the second time in as many minutes and thought to myself I ought to just go home. One more cast and I'd hook the bugger in the keeper and call it quits.

As the odd and homely creation made its final swing across the tail end of the slow run I lifted the rod tip and began to reel it in, accepting failure yet again. And that's when it happened. The line went tight, and for five seconds I was convinced I'd snagged a log, and then the line resonated with tension as it began to cut across the surface of the creek to the opposite side.

I laughed out loud, then the seriousness of my first winter catch on the fly took over. I was suddenly full of fear that at any second the tippet would snap and I'd never even get a glimpse of whatever it was playing tug-of-war at the other end. In the end I found myself struggling with the rod held high and behind me, my left arm stretched out for all it was worth trying to capture a bruiser of a fifteen inch brown, the fish undoubtedly embarrassed by having been fooled by such an unnatural and peculiar fraud.

Since the air temperature was hovering around the twelve degree mark I didn't want to keep the brown out of the water very long. I tossed the fly rod up on the ice. I needed proof. I did my best to snap a couple shots of the humiliated trout which in turn did its best to look away from the camera in shame. All the while laughing out loud to myself like a lunatic. Had anyone been in earshot of the scene they most likely would've been calling the people that hand out the straitjackets. "There's a nut job standing in the half frozen creek. I think he's got an unhealthy brain freeze going on. You better go pull the poor S.O.B. from the water before he hurts himself."

The fish swam back out into the easy current, most likely with an image of that ungodly red thing it had for some reason thought would be a good lunch stuck in its mind, most likely hoping none of the other fish were close enough to see it all unfold. I almost made another cast. Almost. But then I thought the odds of another trout as the temperature was beginning its drop in the same spot on that same weird fly were slim. I figured why ruin the rest of the day by ending the outing with a bunch of empty casts. I'd end it with a fifteen inch brown on a peculiar, but somehow now attractive red Woolly Bugger that had been tied due only to the mysteries of the universe.

I should've made a few more casts. That evening the ice managed to reach from both sides to meet in the middle, and the rest of the winter the trout stayed safely below. Locked under ten inches of ice, while the air struggled to climb to minus twenty above it, I stared out my window for the rest of the winter knowing they were there. It was possible. And Mother Nature was laughing her ass off deciding to close off my opportunities until spring. Irony, it would seem, is a year round catch and release trout stream frozen over all winter. And it stings like frostbite.

Summer Daydreaming at 3am

2:30 A.M. The alarm rouses me from a dead sleep. I quietly move through the house, trying not to wake up my wife and boys. The clank of a coffee cup as I pull it from the cupboard makes me shake my head, half expecting to see a five year old boy appear in the kitchen doorway because of it. I make two cups and spill it everywhere except into the thermos as I try to fill it up. Again, I shake my head. It's 2:35. I should be sleeping.

I walk out into a room off of the back of the house. One containing my fly tying bench, a rustic table with burned images of fish I've caught and have yet to catch, the walls covered in antique fishing tackle and a book shelf made from a cedar tree trunk I pulled out of the creek out back. This is the room where I write and tie flies. A room I escape to when I can't *get out.* There's notes jotted down on a piece of paper on the table, ideas and memories of a summer fishing trip. My eyes move from the notes to the windows. Icicles forming prison bars, the irony making my head shake for the third time in mere minutes. I do a lot of head shaking these days. I grab a magazine and walk out shutting off the light. Time to leave for work.

The truck door won't open, it's frozen shut. I pull and swear under my breath, a tearing noise as the rubber door seal separates from cold painted steel. The seat is as hard as a brick, the brake pedal stiff under my foot. It's fourteen below zero, nothing wants to do its job. As the truck warms up and I wait for a mail slot sized opening to thaw on the windshield, I set my thermos in the cup holder, it rocks side to side. Picking it up, I find the reason to be two flies left there from the last days of warmer weather when I casted beside my father on the West Canada Creek. I hold them up to my face in the dimly illuminated cab and remember standing in the river. The feel of the rocks beneath my boots, the current pushing against my legs in neoprene waders, and the loop of the line. Past the flies I see just enough of an opening in the frost to drive away. I hook the flies on the visor and back out of the driveway.

Leaving my street I cross the first bridge over the Oriskany Creek. If it wasn't for the white of the snow that covers the ice layer separating the creek from the frigid air above it, I wouldn't even know it was there in the pitch black of 2:50am. I think of a past summer day.

Standing on the high bank below the bridge, the butt of my 3wt resting on my toes as I watch my 9yr old son bring in his third fish on his own. He's in his own world. Not asking when we can go home, not talking about video games, not talking at all. Just fishing. I catch myself in the early morning day dream just as my next turn comes up, the truck drifts sideways on a light layer of white powder through another corner, the windshield half thawed now.

The road I drive to work follows the creek for a short distance, passing a pull off that I use every day on my way to work to get in *just a couple casts* when it's not frozen over and when your guides don't freeze up after one cast. I think about warmer days when I'll once again pull off and hurriedly shuffle down the gravel bank and strip line in haste at the water's edge. "Just one smallmouth. Come on, I know you're here. I have to go. Come on, just one bite."

As I drive on, through the mostly defrosted windshield I see nothing but snow banks on both sides and darkness ahead. I turn up the radio, and a song about a river and summer time fills the truck cab. It puts me in a canoe, mid-July, a blue sky. I can feel the sun on the back of my neck. Dragon flies hover inches above the water's surface, bobbing and weaving, dipping to splash down and buzz off in another direction. The motion of the cast relaxes me, the line shooting forward excites, and the bend of the rod as the Bass turns and swims for freedom makes me feel alive. Then a stop sign. The truck slides to a halt pushing slush and snow in front of the tires and I'm back to 2:58am. Reality. Winter sucks.

The First Keeper of the Season

The opening of trout season got a late start. It was an extremely frigid winter, days above zero were outnumbered by the days below, and I'm not just talking a couple degrees below either. To see twenty and thirty below on the thermometer failed to register any shock finally at some point, the shock had instead turned more to just plain resentment. My loathing for the extreme cold had begun while climbing the towers, and by now wiped out any shock and awe that the sub zeros had brought on in the beginning of the season. The creek out my back door is one of only a few in the state that's open to catch and release trout fishing year round, but it was frozen over solid all winter, starting the day after I'd caught my first ever winter brown on the fly. By late March I was a ranting lunatic, permanent brain freeze had set in.

So in the beginning of April when trout season opened and the ice was still hanging as shelves off the banks I found myself on the creek out back jumping from ice shelf to ice chunks casting to fast, high, brown, still too cold water, the occasional iceberg floating by. But the water was more or less open, so with a fly rod I hit the slow water along the banks anyways in protest to the horrendous early season conditions.

Later when the water level finally dropped and the ice was melted away from everywhere but the most shaded bends and banks I found myself on a Saturday wandering the stretch of creek I call my backyard with my fly rod, assessing the changes to the creek done by the massive ice flows at ice out. Huge ice jams of epic proportions had ground their way down stream, changing both the contour of the bottom and the width of the creek in a few places. The creek I knew like the back of my hand would have to be relearned for the new year.

When ice jams full of over foot thick chunks scrape their way downstream from surface to river bottom and bank to bank the aftermath is all you need to see the true strength of nature and realize how small and powerless you really are. Ten foot tall straight cut sand banks were lined on top with small trees that had been flattened to the ground like a steam roller flattening a stand of cattails and the trees strong enough to stand against the bullying ice where stripped of their bark. A combination of shredded and polished tree trunks stood as evidence to the height of the ice flows at the peak. I wondered how any fish big or small could survive such an ordeal without being crushed and scraped downstream against the bottom.

I hadn't figured I'd catch anything, and I hadn't caught anything. Not even a tug. Not even a flash of scales as I walked carelessly along the bank actually hoping to scare a fish just to see something move. I'd made my way about a mile up the curving and meandering water way inspecting new downed trees and new cobblestone skinny water flats. I stared in amazement at a stretch that was once a slow run with overhanging Willows on the far bank, now not a tree remained. The creek must have been a few feet wider, all the Willows washed down river leaving a barren and featureless run.

I witnessed the damage the ice had done under the train bridge in town where it peeled and bent a piece of half inch thick plate steel backwards in the current, which now looked to me like the most perfect current break for smallmouths to wait in ambush behind. I finally found myself standing below the concrete spillway directly behind my house, the orange canoe resting on its side two hundred yards away in the back yard now in view.

I stood there and made a few casts letting a streamer wash down the concrete and get pushed to the bottom in the rolling froth, hoping as it bumped its way across the rocky bottom that something, anything, might decide it was a meal. Nothing did. Still not a bad day by any means, but a fishless day no less. I hooked the streamer into the keeper above the cork and as I began to wade across the creek to make my way up to the house gravel popped as a car pulled off the road. A young guy probably in his mid-twenties got out, gathered a spinning rod and a bait bucket and made his way to the water's edge. I waved, he nodded, and I continued across the current to the far bank.

That's when I saw it. In the open, where almost anyone could see it, from the road even, was a large set of antlers resting on the rocky bank. I looked back, there was no way it couldn't be seen from where the car was parked, let alone where he was baiting his hook. If the water was lower, if it had been easier to get to than having to cross the creek, I was sure what I'd just found would have been found and taken home as a prize by now, someone else's trophy from a day on the water. But I'd found it. It was mine.

The deer must have washed down river with the ice flows judging by where it came to rest at the high water mark. A skeleton held together by stiff leather and sinew and not much else, I inspected it for some kind of evidence of what could have caused the animals death. There wasn't enough of a hide left to find a wound, and without digging around, from what I could see there were no arrow heads or bullet damage on any of the ribs or front shoulders where a hunter's aim would've mortally wounded it, so it was all guess as to its final moments. Had it been shot and never found during the fall, only to die next to the creek and be washed away with the rising water levels of spring? Did it attempt a crossing during the winter only to break through and drown, caught in a frozen watery grave? I'd never know.

I grabbed an antler thinking the skull would fall away but nature hadn't had enough time to finish the job. I looked over my shoulder at the young fisherman. If he'd seen what I was looking at he wasn't showing it. Probably caught up in the whole "Come on, just one bite, just one fish please" thing in his head. I had to give nature a little more time with it before I could take the gorgeous rack home, but surely someone else would claim it if I left it where it laid. Or the other chance would be the water would rise again and wash it downstream, lost. I dragged it higher up the bank and behind a large log, then using the only thing I had, 6lb tippet, I tied the antlers off to a sapling thinking that if the water rose it would have a chance at least of remaining.

The next week I walked the hundred and some odd yards from my back door to find that the skull had separated aided by time and scavenging rodents. I turned over rotting leaves with my boot and buried the skull, leaving it to the worms, bugs, and beetles to finish cleaning it up and left it there, checking it from time to time over the next month or so. When I finally brought it up to the house I pressure washed it and soaked it in bleach for a couple days. Then I gave it a new home.

My writing and tying room is full of things I've found while out fishing. An old Horrocks-Ibbotson fiberglass spinning rod found broken and propped against a tree on the Mohawk River leans in the corner against a beaver chewed tree dragged up and out of a ravine in another place. A shelf full of old liquor bottles with fishing themes. A cedar tree trunk hauled out of the Oriskany Creek on my way to work one morning. Old fly reels found at garage sales and in attics and basements. Another cedar trunk figured and smooth pulled from the Schroon River in the Adirondacks. A good number of old rods and reels pulled down from my neighbors rafters that he hadn't fished since the sixties. Sycamore stands as legs for my tying bench, and old flies and lures pulled from tree branches find a final resting place stuck in an old cork handle. Old pocket knives of various makes and sizes collected over the years tell stories only I can hear. Pieces of drift would and relics litter the room, all radiating memories.

I don't have any fish mounts in the room, which some people would think odd since I'm such a fanatical angler and have a room dedicated to it. I do however have a ten point buck skull with a beautiful rack on a shelf surrounded by fishing paraphernalla. I don't even hunt. A visitor to our house said to me upon seeing the skull in the room "Oh, I didn't know you hunt too?" To which I replied, "No, you're right I don't. That's a fishing trophy. It was a keeper from this past spring." Henry David Thoreau said "Many men go fishing all of their lives not knowing that it is not fish that they are after." Now I'm not sure that it's ten point bucks resting in peace after the spring floods have receded that we're looking for, but I'm not saying they don't have something to do with it either.

Story Stik

I'd been up all night working a twelve hour midnight shift. I hadn't slept since yesterday afternoon. My eyes itched, my reflexes were somewhat slowed, my mind might've slightly drifted towards auto pilot, and it could've if I hadn't been waiting for this day all week. Blue skies, a calm breeze, and a box full of streamers the size of hot wings that I'd been tying for the past two months waited for me outside, the streamer box and my new 7wt dubbed *"Story Stik"* laid on the hood of the truck.

I take the naming of a custom rod as important business, akin to the naming of a boat, maybe only more important to me since I've never *owned* a boat. Just like Forest Gump's boat "Jenny," I believe the name of a custom rod should evoke fond memories, perhaps relate to the owners life somehow in deep seeded ways or in the least make everyone, merely at the sight of the name inscribed on the rod, want to give it a cast. I think you *can* go overboard. So in choosing a name you probably shouldn't go over the top, picking names of famous swords like Excalibur. But what you're shooting for is something that makes you feel, well, not like Apollo Creed dancing in front of Ivan Drago in a glittery Uncle Sam suit and top hat in Rocky IV. That's just asking to get skunked, and nobody likes a cocky fly fisherman, so reel in the ego pal. You're going more for Rocky at the top of the steps surrounded by cheering and pumped up kids. That's just class. Good vibes. You can still get skunked and feel good about it, somewhat anyways.

The perfect example of a great name would be our buddy Doug's 9wt. He named it "Love Machine" which now that I think about it, I have no idea what fond memories it stirs up or how it relates to his life, so that could throw my entire naming spiel right out the window. I will say though that Doug is the only person I know in our circle of friends that loves to fish more than me and he's damn good at it, so perhaps if fly fishing is his first love then the name is the best he could've ever come up with, as good or better than mine actually. And I also guess it's entirely possible to over analyze such trivial things as naming a fly rod.

I picked Story Stik for obvious reasons, but when I texted it late one night to JP I spelled it the right way. JP being the artist chose to spell it "Story *Stik*" because, being the artist, he realized it looked cooler. But in all honesty, if I choose the name because I use my fly rods as writing tools like a mechanic uses wrenches, then the perfect hidden irony lies in any of my first drafts of my stories scribbled in various note books scattered about. You'd see in these that spell check was indeed one of the greatest inventions ever and then realize that the misspelled name fits even more than the meaning of the name in the first place.

The night before through a series of texts, JP and I had tried to put together a time and place to meet up to hit the water together, but in the end, it looked like he'd be on his way to Maine in search of brook trout, while I couldn't stray far from home. The opening weekend of our town's Little League season, including the parade of all the teams complete with t-ballers hurling candy at friends on the curb, a speech by the mayor on the pristine manicured field, and first games are *not* to be missed when you've got both your young sons swinging aluminum bats in search of glory. But that was tomorrow, and this was today. And I could sleep next week.

At 8:40am, after Holly left for work, and Jake and Carter stepped onto the bus, I went into fish mode. The fact that I'd been up since 4pm the day before and worked all night had no bearing on anything. The sun was up, and I was free to do as I pleased. I had a new fly rod and a fly box full of enough feathers and fur to make a PETA activist vomit their vegetarian dinner all over their anything but leather shoes so I took off.

I beat feet and found myself leaving the truck in a parking area and hurrying down a paved walking trail, net on my back and nine foot six inches of fly rod at my side. I left the paved path where the Barge Canal spilled over a small dam and flowed through woods until it mixed and

61

its waters became one with the current of the Mohawk River. I love history, and the areas we fish here are full of it. What we call the Barge Canal now is the final end game of what was once the Erie Canal that you read of in your history books in school, and the Mohawk River was named after the fierce Mohawk Indians that once lived in our part of the country. But I wasn't here for history, I was here to make my own.

The river was just right for wading, and this early in the spring I didn't have to worry so much about busting through ground cover and snagging the fly rod every two steps. But it wouldn't be long before the foliage would be full and the ground would be all but covered like a jungle, nearly impassable on foot, the only hope of fishing the river being from a canoe. I stepped into the river, stripped fly line, and as it moved with the water in loose coils at my knees, I made my first cast.

Now I've never liked big heavy rods. Long before I ever picked up a fly rod, my weapon of choice had always been light and ultra-light spinning rods. Medium to heavy bass rods always felt like clubs in my hand. Likewise, up to this point my choice in fly rods had been a 5wt and my short 3wt. I wanted a heavier rod to throw big streamers which is why I had JP build me the 7wt, but at the same time I'd been apprehensive. Would I like it once I had it? I was afraid of it feeling like a stiff tree branch in my hand and not wanting to use it because of it. It would look cool on the wall, but I wanted a rod to fish.

My first cast put those fears to rest. It felt natural, the rod bent like a reed sways in the wind, and the line flowed through the guides like silk. I may not have hooked a fish on the Mohawk that morning, but I was hooked on the new 7wt. Like a crackhead needs a fix, I needed another cast. And another. And another. I told myself the lie all fisherman tell themselves, *just one more cast and then I'll go* at least 20 times before I actually headed for my truck and a different creek.

Fifteen minutes later I found myself standing in a bend of the Oriskany Creek, just above where it too flowed into the Mohawk. The Oriskany Creek flows south to north for about thirty miles give or take and not only have I fished it since I was a kid, but it runs through my back yard, past the little league field, which can be convenient if you catch my drift, and just outside of the village it flows into the Mohawk. There's a lot more history here to be told about wars and people killing each other, but the fish... The creek holds great browns, both stocked and wild, and brawling bronze backs. Smallmouth that aren't afraid to view most anything as a meal to be eaten or an intruder to be crushed.

Standing in a tight curve, in a current passing at about waist level, I tossed a black bunny leach about four inches long on a size 1/0 hook into the top of the curve, where the water darkened to a deep clear green in contrast to the shallow sandy bottom on which I stood only feet away. The streamer landed only a couple inches or so from the cut-out sand bank rising ten feet on the opposite side of the creek and I let it sink and travel with the current until I guessed its lead dumb bell eyes had taken it far enough down to start my retrieve in the faces of the fish that just had to be there in my mind. Five slow strips. The water was still cold this early in spring, the fish would still be slow, possibly lethargic. Five slow strips and then a pause, and on the next strip, the line went tight, and as I lifted the rod tip, the rod bent and danced, the line cutting the water back and forth.

Twice I brought smallmouths to hand that had the markings of the wicked warriors they were, vertical black stripes and blotches against deep bronze scales like the camo make-up of a brutal special forces operator on a mission to unleash guerilla warfare in the form of violent ambush. After sending a picture to JP of the better of the two a text came back almost immediately, asking why I didn't call him, and calling me a less than pleasant name as only friends can do. It had something to do with the male anatomy and a problem you'd visit a doctor for. I couldn't come up with anything good to fire back. It turned out that I'd read the last text the evening before wrong. Maine was only a suggestion. Moral of the story...Quit texting, make the call, and use your voice.

I met JP in his drive way 30 minutes later, his jet boat already behind the Jeep, and we were off, heading north. The first idea was tanked as we found the boat launch was closed, not a soul around, a locked gate. We hung our heads but refused to give up so easily.

And so it was that we found ourselves motoring across Delta Lake and making for the inlet where the Mohawk feeds the massive manmade body of water where the town of Delta once stood. In the fall they lower the reservoir level and you can walk across some of it and see the old cobblestone foundations of houses long gone. You can also find lures snagged in them which is always a fun way to pass the time. My brother has found entire fishing rods and tackle boxes, making you picture canoes wrong side up, and dog paddling.

Making it all the way across the lake to the mouth of the Mohawk we found shallow, clear water in the channel that was the temporary end of the river and would become the lake in a few hundred yards, only to become the river once again below a dam. I strung up another black bunny leach as JP took a seat and steadied the boat with the oars. As I made my third or fourth cast to the narrow, dark channel along the river bank, I spotted the massive carp swimming along in the dark depths and gasped to JP "Holy crap, look at those huge carp right in front of us!"

I lowered the anchor to the shallow rocky bottom and JP rummaged through his fly box and handed me something small and greenish. Buggy looking, it resembled something either a carp would eat or something you'd find in your handkerchief after you blew your nose. I tied it on. Naturally, the carp disappeared almost instantly, but we knew they were there, so hope was at the end of every cast.

At some point I shamed JP into leaving the oars and taking up his rod, telling him that I felt like a piece of crap doing all the fishing. He's the guy that's just happy to be in the boat and at the oars steadying it for a clear cast. I'm the guy that feels awkward when someone else is doing all the work, but somehow we get along just peachy out on the water. As he stood on the bow platform, casting and talking, his rod jerked, he made a motion with the rod like someone yanking their hand out of a bear trap at the last minute, and the line flew from the water, sans fly. He turned to me with a look of "*What the hell?*" and could hardly get the words out of his mouth. "I saw gills flare, a mouth suck in the fly, and the fly was gone!" I thought it was cool as anything. A tiger musky had paid us a visit. Jordan suddenly looked upset. "That should have been *your* fish." I told him don't sweat it. It was cool enough that it happened.

Later, as we loaded the boat back onto the trailer, as JP replayed the story again, I told him it was cool, I seriously thought it was cool. He wasn't even going for a toothy fish, he was loaded for carp at that point, yet he lost his carp fly to a fish at the top of the food chain that afternoon. I told him I honestly wasn't let down, that it was just more motivation. I also thought it was better that he got to go to bed that night seeing it replay in his head over and over. The flaring of the gills, the inhaling of the fly, the pop of the line. I was glad it happened to him...Because I couldn't have slept that night if it had happened to me.

In Pursuit of Pike

10:30pm. I sit in silence under the light of my tying bench, my wife and kids asleep, the rest of the house dark. Bear paces back and forth from one end of the house to the other, his nails clacking on wood floors, stressing out over whether he should be curled up on his dog bed in our bedroom where Holly's sleeping or sitting by me in my room as I tie yet another bait fish streamer meant to entice the slime missiles I've made it my goal to catch on the fly this year. I've tied most likely upwards of thirty streamers, all different sizes and colors, and lost three of them to my intended targets, but not one, yet, has brought me my northern pike I'm so intent on hooking into and landing this year.

In fifteen minutes I'll have to be out the door and on my way to work, a loud and grungy factory midnight shift waits ready to greet me with open arms and broken equipment needing to be repaired. These will be my last quiet minutes of today. In the driveway my Toyota sits patiently, the heavy orange plastic canoe strapped to the rack. The fighting butt of my 7wt rests on the dash while the tip nearly reaches out to the tailgate through the back window. I haven't even left for work yet but I'm already geared up to chase fish first thing in the morning.

As I pull out of my neighborhood my eye lids are already heavy. I put all my windows down and turn on the radio. Cranking up the tunes to keep myself alert, the speakers blare as Motley Crue shouts at the devil. The cool wind and the wailing guitar wake me up and bring my mind back to a younger me. Long hair, ripped blue jeans, I remember crouching in the tall grass on the edge of the pond next door where I grew up as I stalked largemouths with a spinning rod. Life was easier, and given the fact that I've been skunked for the past week and a half as I've pursued long toothy game fish, the fishing seemed easier back then too. The song ends and I'm snapped back to reality as something less energetic flows from the speakers and I search the stations for more energy and more memories.

The night drags by painfully at work. Thankfully nothing's breaking on the graveyard shift, but unfortunately nothing's breaking on the graveyard shift. I've got nothing to do but watch the clock and think of pike waiting in ambush in weed beds and under log jams. Eight hours feels more like twelve. When a foreman asks me if I *actually* want to

66

work twelve a half hour before the end of my shift I fight back laughter and politely answer *hell no.* By the time I'm standing in the locker room I can't get out of my coveralls fast enough and out the door. I smile an impatient and fake smile as I wait in line at the time clock to punch out. But I can see the orange canoe on my truck above the other vehicles in the parking lot through the doors. You guys need to move faster, you just don't understand. *I have places to be.*

While I fought to keep my eyes open all night, or all *morning* if that's how you want to look at it, the fresh air and the sun filled sky have given me my second wind. I've come to count on this second wind lately as if it were a couple extra hours on the clock. It's not of course, as ridiculous as day light savings time is, this is no different. Stealing an hour off one end of the day and putting it on the other end to make the day longer only works if you're crazy or stupid. Or a fly fishing addict. What happens lately is that I use up my second wind for all it's worth, then stretch it out a bit more, then sleep a couple hours before working all night again. About every week and a half I crash and sleep for an entire day. I don't feel any better after that, and then I start the cycle over again. But I'm fishing.

As I pass the guard shack on my way out the gate I turn on the radio, this time for nothing more than something to make the drive go by faster. I hang my arm out the window and watch the front of the canoe vibrate, it juts out over the windshield and cuts the wind like a wedge as Tom Petty is running down a dream through the truck's speakers. I turn it up, my foot pushes the gas pedal down a little farther and the fur and feathers of the streamers stuck in the dash dance in the wind blowing through the cab.

I know I only should stay an hour or two as I push off from the bank and the boat glides out into the barely noticeable current of the slow river, so I hope to make this a quick cast and catch adventure so that I can get some sleep before doing it all over again tonight. That's nothing more than my lack of sleep lately making me delusional. I cast to every fishy looking undercut bank. I cast to every side of every submerged tree I pass, to every drop off, and I strike out each time. Not so much as a follow or even the movement of water being displaced from below to hint that I might be any closer to my victory. I finally find myself along the very stretch of river that I lost my first streamers to weeks ago when I realized that I would indeed need some type of a steel leader or extremely heavy mono to fend off the vicious teeth of the water's apex predator.

I inspect my streamer. It looks great. Perfect. It looks like a small fish, the only thing missing is the neon sign with the blinking arrow pointing to it that reads "*Eat Here.*"

I replay the fish from this spot in my mind weeks ago when I was so close to my win yet so far away. I see the white and red streamer slap the water and begin to sink. As I strip it once and it jerks forward and then turns slightly to the side, the fish it appears, like a serial killer stepping from the shadows, it's suddenly just there suspended where it wasn't only a second ago. Launching, it covers the distance in the blink of an eye, perhaps faster. Gills flare, the mouth opens, and the fly's inhaled. As the fish turns back to return to its ambush position I strip set and pull up on the rod. The hook is set. The pike fights to continue its turn, the rod bends. I smile and breathe out a "Yes!" My buddy Brian sits in the other end and as I hear him say "There ya go!" the fish gives a head shake and just like that the rod goes limp and the fish goes in another direction with my streamer. The game is over. I stand in the canoe as my heart pounds and just stare. So close.

This time I'm ready, a steel leader between the streamer and the mono is my defense. I cast. Just like the first time. It slaps the water and begins to sink. Just like the first time. I give it a couple good strips, it looks perfect as it jerks forward and pauses, showing off the profile of a wounded bait fish just right as it hovers in place and then begins to sink again. Nothing. I stay in this spot for what seems like an hour. Casting. Pleading. *Come and get it. Take a bite. Take a swipe. Take a look. Just show me something and I can go home and go to sleep.* But nothing.

It's bad enough that I haven't caught anything in a week and a half, let alone a northern, but it's not for a lack of trying. I want to feel something on the end of the line so bad at that moment that I almost think it wouldn't be so bad if I hooked myself on the back cast. At least then I'd feel some tension on the line.

Pulling back onto the pavement I turn on the radio for the ride home. It looks like I'll only be getting about three hours of sleep today since the plan of staying for an hour or so was shot about four hours ago. I hit the search button and it stops on the next station. I know the guitar. The Dire Straits, So Far Away. Streamers stuck in the dash seem to sway to the sad tune.

Oriskany Creek Logic

I stand in a stretch of the Oriskany Creek, staring down the Weeping Willow that's attached to the other end of my fly line, a few tugs leading to a few furious shakes, leaves falling to the water and floating on the current as I make the decision to just break off the fly. I pull the line tight, tighter still, until it finally pops...The fly falls to the water and disappears downstream with the current, my eyes follow it as the current takes it away, no longer snagged in the willow. That's about my luck. I shake my head, laugh at myself, and inspect my fly box, wondering which one I'll most likely lose next.

I tie on a black leech pattern, nothing more than a strip of rabbit fur, and make a cast, narrowly missing the same branches that moments earlier dragged a four letter word across my lips. The fly lands against the cutout sand bank and rolls down into the water. A few seconds later the line is tight, the rod arching overhead, a fish fighting for yards like a football player making slow progress with another dragging from his leg. When the fight's over I cradle a gorgeous greenish bronze smallmouth with the dark striped markings. I remove the hook from its mouth, admire the fish for another quick moment and then lower it back to the cool water. With a kick and a splash it glides off to deeper shadows and I'm left with water and sand speckled on my face. I figure it's like the fish saying *here's mud in your eye*. I suppose I deserve it.

The Oriskany Creek is known as brown trout water, and it is. But I'm a horrible trout fisherman, unless you're talking about the wild brook trout that I hunt in remote Adirondack streams. Most of them haven't seen an artificial fly, they just don't know any better. But here in the Oriskany the browns seem to know when I'm here and let the bass, the fall fish, and the creek chubs take the bait instead, no pun intended. I don't mind in the least. Time on the creek is time on the creek, no matter what I find at the end of my line, if I find anything at the end at all. There's carp in places too, but carp I've come to find are jerks. I don't bother much with them, and when I do I fail and lie saying I wasn't bothering with them. I'm a fly fisherman, a decent liar at best.

But I do hook a brown every now and then to be sure. Sometimes I feel like they might feel sorry for me and reluctantly take a fly just to ease their guilt. I'll take them honest or I'll let them think they're doing me a favor and play along with their ruse. We shake hands during the release, I make my way one direction and they swim off in another, both of us getting a glimpse of another world if for only a few seconds.

The fish and I, we have an understanding. They understand I'm trying to catch them, and I understand they don't want to be caught. Some days we balance each other out well. On many others the balance seems to be tipped in their favor. I never hold it against them. They're just fish after all, and I'm only human.

Priorities and Avoiding Skunks

Coming off the midnight shift I came home and showered, trying to scrub off the smell of work. Not so much because I smelled, I've gotten used to the smell of the alloy plant, but because I didn't want to be reminded of work every time I raised my arms near my face for the rest of the day. I wanted to forget it.

The one good thing about quitting a life on the road working in the great outdoors for a life at home sweating in a dirty, smelly alloy plant is also the one and only goal I had when I took the job. I get to see my kids grow up. So after showering and throwing a bowl of cereal down my throat I met my oldest son's fourth grade class in town to go on a tour of Fort Stanwix, then on to the Oriskany Battle Field for a picnic and a history lesson. This is stuff I never got to do while working on the road. The alloy plant may weigh on my mind as *not my kind of job,* but outside of the job things are better.

Come to think of it, it's odd, the job change. I feel like either place, working on the road or stuck in the plant is a prison sentence, stealing away my life a day at a time. If this current job is like being stuck in a dark and dirty prison surrounded by bad vibes and bad attitudes with wardens looking over your shoulder, then the cell tower job on the road was like the inmates you see on the side of the road cutting grass and picking up trash. You're still in prison, but at least you get to see the outside world go by. I'm torn on which works out better for me.

Fishing on the other hand has taken a huge nose dive compared to the four years I spent on the road when I fished nearly seven days a week sometimes. My longest stretch of non-stop casting was *thirty-nine* days for crying out loud. So now days, when I have an opening, I've got to make the best of it. As the teachers tried to load kids back onto the school bus, their voices raised and the chaos of children running in all directions playing tag and just creating general mischief, the idea of trying to herd cats came to mind. Then as the bus pulled away I knew this was my time, my window. With my beat up orange canoe on top of the truck and fly rods assembled and stretching from the dash and out the back window I pointed the truck to water roughly forty-five minutes south in hopes of finding a pike willing to take a streamer on the 7wt.

Pulling into one of the only access points I could find for the Sangerfield River on the maps I was disappointed and let down. The water was the color of my sons chocolate milk at breakfast with sticks and leaves added in for a little texture instead of marshmallows. There was fifty minutes of valuable fishing time *lost*. I sat staring at the water only a few yards away, my fly rods close enough to brush my arm as I turned the steering wheel, and I closed my eyes, trying to imagine myself on the map, and what else was close enough to stop at on my way back. I remembered a small lake that I'd driven past probably a hundred times but never fished, and it was only a couple miles out of the way. What was a couple more miles at this point? Well, it was a couple more miles is all. Gravel flew as I put the truck in reverse. The fishing portion of the day wasn't totally lost yet.

It was hot now. About eighty-four. The sun beat down, and the water wasn't deep. As I paddled for the lily pads I'd picked as my first target the wind began to pick up to a little more than the nice breeze it had been and I fought it as it tried to push the long orange plastic vessel where I didn't want to go. Three times I let the wind drift me past the pads as I cast a streamer to the edge hoping for the bass that *had* to be sheltering in the shade to blast out and crush it. Three times nothing. The change to a popper was nothing more than a *what do I have to lose* attempt in all honesty. Kind of like coming to this lake in the first place really. When I get in the *what do I have to lose* frame of mind, all bets are off, anything can happen. Again, several casts and nothing. But standing in the canoe, trying to spot a likely taker, I spotted lots of small cruising dark shapes. Bluegill, sunfish, little pan fish that would normally take anything, sometimes even a bare hook.

Another *what do I have to lose* fly change found me tying on a cricket imitation on my 7wt. I questioned myself if I'd gone insane in the heat, going after hand sized pan fish with a 7wt fly rod. I didn't question it again for the next twenty something casts, as nearly each one brought in another brightly colored hand sized slab that fought like much bigger fish for a meal they raced to from all directions as it hit the water, like a bunch of dogs waiting for a tennis ball to be thrown, all of them scrambling to get it first.

I looked at the time and decided that I had to put down the rod and pick up the paddle if I wanted to make it to our youngest sons Little League game. It was tough but when I told myself this was the last cast, for the first time in my life possibly, I think it actually *was*. Loading the canoe back on the truck I was happy. I left home hoping for a pike. Then I downgraded to hoping for bass. Then I settled on pan fish and never looked back.

I don't believe I'm a good fisherman at all. I know plenty of guys who would have been plain pissed off because of how the day unfolded and would have never even bothered with the little worm stealers. If I'm a good fisherman in any way at all, it's because I'm happy to just be out, and I'll make the best of any fishing I can find. It's honestly the only thing in life I seem to be able to look on the bright side of when things aren't going great.

On my way back home I passed a spot on the Oriskany Creek that I haven't fished in about 5 years. I used to fish it on my lunches when I was a blacksmith, a story for another time. Knowing I had about ten minutes to spare, I pulled in and selected the short 3wt from the dash board line-up. With a tiny olive Woolly Bugger tied on a tiny size 14 hook I made two casts and in two casts I brought to hand two small browns. When I say small I mean about four to five inches small. But in a creek that gets stocked over a wild population I figured at least I'd caught the wild ones. They just don't stock them that small. That was that. Some days it's better to be lucky than good.

As I pulled into the ball field lot, stones popped under rubber and a cloud of dust settled on the hood and windshield. I walked to the bleachers just in time to see Carter, my five year old, step up to bat. Nothing like perfect timing.

Sitting there I realized what a horrible headache I had. I bought a bottle of water at the concession stand, my first drink of anything since sometime around 5am at work. And then I was reminded that I hadn't gone to sleep yet since working the midnight shift...it was now 6pm. I told myself I needed to get better at the whole taking care of myself thing. But it's fishing after all. And while I lived on the road I thought it would be diners and fast food that did me in. I'll take done in by fishing compared to done in by high cholesterol any day.

Fly Rods Are Not Found in the Lawn Care Department

It's an older bike. Not an old Pan Head or Shovel, just a fifteen year old Sportster. But it looks like it's thirty years old as it sits in the drive way, rust breaking through chrome, chipped, black paint covered in dust and a yellow layer of spring pollen. A speedometer that doesn't work, and a missing air cleaner cover. Fogged and faded orange turn signals. A crude but functional sissy bar is what my pack containing my waders, my fly box, and the fly rod tube is strapped to with a couple miss matched bungee cords. The exhaust is missing the heat shields, in reality the only reason the waders are rolled up in the pack. I'd hate to burn a hole in my waders as I sat at a traffic light waiting for the green, while contemplating the time the red light was stealing from my allotted fishing time budget. Forget the strange looks I'd get from the cars around me, if it would save me time getting ready at stream side, it would be worth it.

As I tighten my old blue metal flake helmet, one that makes me think of the old circus acts, a nut job getting shot out of a cannon, I look at the lawn. Yea, yea. It needs to be mowed. But it's early. It's still soaked in dew from the night before. It needs time to dry before I fire up my least favorite thing in the world second only to a job. The mower. So there's no better way to wait for the lawn to dry than to go fishing.

The bike chugs along and I remember how when I used to really be into riding these things, when I built them, when I had a nice bike, how everyone would always pour over the idea that when they rode it cleared their minds. They were free. I never felt that way. And this ride reminds me. Riding, I have nothing to do *but* think. My mind far from clear. I think about how long I have to chuck streamers and chase fins with the 7wt before I've run out of time to get the stupid lawn cut.

I pass through the old air base that we now call an *industrial park* and pass by acres upon acres of short, manicured, green and sprawling grass and think to myself what a waste of time. All that time spent burning gas and making laps, for something that's just going to grow back again tomorrow. Something that its sole purpose is to grow. All that time in the seat, your ears ringing at the end of the day...Wasting valuable fishing time. I'm suddenly glad my lawn is the size of my living

76

room. If it were any smaller I could probably cut it with scissors and rake it into a zip lock bag.

When we first moved into suburbia hell I was a little perturbed to say the least that we had so little land, such a small yard compared to the old place with the dairy farm across the road. Now I'll admit that the small yard isn't so bad because it doesn't take very long to cut it. But I still hate mowing when I should be fishing.

During the twenty minute ride I've got plenty of time to think about all the things that keep me off the water lately. It's been a tough season on me so far. The past four years I fished so much that I never considered what it would be like to ever go back to a normal job where I couldn't fish new waters five days a week. This year, coming back home and working a normal job, midnight shifts, the boy's ball games, it's all a bit over whelming. As I picture the damn lawn mower waiting for me back at the house again I pitch the bike over to the right hard through a corner and twist on the throttle.
The water's close. Closer if I speed up.

At the water there's a back pack, an empty rod tube, and an old blue metal flake helmet sitting on the rocks as I wade out under the old stone bridge and into the sunlight below the dam. I forget about the lawn. What was meant to be an hour or so swinging the 7wt has become nearly four hours of the graceful bend and flex of the rod, of the strip of the line, the jerk and pause of the streamer. A couple follows, a slash and a missed strike, and four hours later I'm back on the bike heading for a lawn that my wife says needs to be cut. But for nearly four hours it was forgotten.

I stop once more before making it home to cast into a hole on a creek that almost never lets me down. For another twenty minutes I forget about the lawn. What does it matter? It's still growing. It'll always be there. The fish, they move around. The smallmouth fights hard and we shake hands at the end. The fish congratulates me on winning the fight, but as a last jab as not to be totally defeated, it winks at me, and asks, "So how's that lawn mowing coming along?" He breaks free from my grasp and I can hear him laughing under water as he disappears back under the cutout bank where there's no lawn to be mowed. Ever.

I think I'd be better off just living in the middle of a field. Fields, you know, don't need to be mowed. They're fields. If that Scottish guy that pushes the lawn fertilizer on TV ever shows up on *my lawn* and tells me to *"Feed your grass man. Feed it!"* I'm punching him square in the nose. Then we're going fishing.

There's a Fishing Magazine in My Tool Box

The living room floor's a battle field. Green army men and tan army men stand toe to toe, rifles trained on each other, the wounded and the dead lie everywhere. For a short while it looked as though the tans would prevail against stacked odds, but then there was a swing in morale as a green sharp shooter lowered their numbers one by one from a hidden position in a pile of Lincoln Logs. The tans were in retreat, victory looked all but certain... Then the Lego ninjas showed up. Like tornados sweeping out across a prairie the Lego ninjas laid all before them to waste, no mercy was given. Bodies lie everywhere, the battle field now quiet and still.

Hard plastic jabs into the underside of my foot as I step though the carnage. Grimacing in pain I stumble and little plastic soldiers are scattered, sliding under the couch to become MIA until the next time the vacuum is run. I mutter under my breath. Moments ago Carter asked if he could play Lego Star Wars on the PlayStation and I told him he needed to clean up the army men first. He's now in his bed room crying because he didn't see why he needed to pick them up. "There's too *many*! I'll *never* be done! It's *not fair*! You *hate* me!" I've heard this before. He'll work it out in his room, reappear with red eyes and pick up his toys. He's six.

I retreat from the battle to my bathroom downstairs. The reading room. I grab a magazine from a stack and flip through the pages for the next ten minutes, a six year old wailing in the background about picking up toys. Life is unfair. He thinks he's knows, but he has no idea, he's six. The magazine takes me to the salt flats of some far off Caribbean island and images of permit and bone fish turn the upset child into white noise in the background. I wish I could somehow find my way to a salt flat in the near future but it's nothing but a dream at this point. Life is too hectic, I don't have the vacation time at work. Money is always less than what it needs to be. Yea, Carter's right, it's not fair. But at least I have fishing magazines in the bathroom, life could be worse.

Later after the boys are in bed and Holly's on the couch watching some show I have no interest in, I realize that the midnight shift is approaching fast. I've got just enough time to make a sandwich, gather up all the trash and get it out to the curb, and Holly reminds me that it's snowing. It'd be nice if I shoveled the drive way before I left so it wasn't so bad in the morning she says. I make my sandwich. I put the trash out to the curb, trying to balance the cans on the built up ridge of dirty snow left at the end of the drive way by the plows during the day. I survey the scene. Yea, I should shovel. But I've got four wheel drive. I can blast through and shovel in the morning when I get home before she leaves for work.

Back in my room upstairs surrounded by fly tying paraphernalia and fishing books and magazines I'm leaned back on the couch with my feet on the coffee table. My laptop is there, opened and ready, I know I have stories to finish, and a book that's been two years in the making still not done. But I'm just not feeling it. I grab a magazine from a pile on the floor and flip through an article on a pike trip to northern Canada. I hear Holly's voice in the back ground, something about the drive way. I study a picture of a huge forty- plus inch pike with a mangled streamer hanging off its jaw and utter a low "Uh huh" to whatever it was she said. She'll find in the morning that she also has four wheel drive, and most likely, she'll be using it to get out of the driveway. I have fishing magazines in my room.

The midnight shift drags on through the early morning. For an hour I'll have nothing to do, plagued by boredom until suddenly I get a call to three different broken down machines all at once. Grease, grit, puddles of hydraulic fluid and broken off bolts, it's one of those nights, or since it's 2am, I guess it's one of those mornings. I finally get caught up, there's time to breath, the building is a buzz of loud rackets, the machines sounding as well tuned as a bunch of buckets full of rocks rolling down a hill, but they're running none the less. I'm thinking about summer, about casting a popper to the lily pads on the family farm and the huge bass I got on the 7wt as I plunk my second quarter into the coffee machine. Before I can hit all the buttons the page tone on the loud speaker goes off again, and I hear once more "Maintenance man to the Orbit Saws." Damn.

Those saws are the last things you want to get called to for anything, much less a break down. That end of the building, those machines set in place back in 1962, it's the darkest, greasiest, most wore out and blatantly unmaintained corner of the entire plant. It's where old machines and young men go to die. It's like Grandma's house...It's dark, and it smells funny.

As the coffee machine fills the paper cup I think in my head what tools I might need for the possibilities of what could be broken. I walk back to my tool box and set a white paper cup of steaming hot coffee covered in dirty finger prints on the top of the box. I shake my head and scowl, I don't want to go get elbow deep in these greasy contraptions. I'm just not feeling it, I've got three hours to go, but in my head I've already clocked out. I open a drawer. Yea, I have a fishing magazine in my tool box.

Pan Fish Epiphanies

The kid was drowning worms on the bank a mere forty feet from where I was standing in the water casting out to the rocks on the opposite side with a small popper. It was one of those marginal fishing days. It was hot. Nothing, including the fish wanted to move much. Except the pan fish of course.

The kid's bobber was resting off to the side in a shallow pool, out of the current where he only had to make minimal corrections to keep it positioned where he wanted it. The bobber bounced a couple times and then traveled about a foot and stopped again. It repeated this a couple times before it finally dipped below the surface and the boy set the hook.

As he was reeling in his spinning rod my chugging popper vanished with a plunking sound and setting the hook the 3wt bent and vibrated with what I was sure was another bluegill or rock bass just like the ten previous. Just like what I and the young boy on the bank knew was on his line too. He hoisted the fish up the bank, rod arched above his head, and once again... "Awww come on, I hate these things. I want a bass." He removed the hook and threw the fish back to the water. I smiled as my own pan fish came into view a few feet out.

Forty years. In forty years what the hell have I really learned? A bunch of clichés are what come to mind. "When it rains it pours." "No news is good news." "Actions speak louder than words." "The acorn doesn't fall far from the tree." "All work and no play makes Jack a dull boy." "An idle mind is the devils playground." "Shit happens." Sometimes "The writing is on the wall." "Money can't buy happiness." And most importantly "A bad day fishing is better than a good day at work."

When my Grandfather and I would sit out on that little peninsula at the lake on the farm, drowning worms all day long, watching boobers get pulled back and forth, bounce up and down, sit motionless for hours on the glass like surface of the still water, I was that kid sometimes. I'd reel in bluegill after bluegill just wanting that bass, or worse, I'd reel in empty hook after empty hook. The tiny pan fish were

82

always hard at work down below stripping the worms off piece by piece, bite by bite like professional pick pockets. Grandpa wasn't immune, sometimes he'd be going through the exact same thing on his side of the peninsula. Only as he watched his bobber wander lazily to the left, then wander lazily to the right, hardly a jiggle, hardly a ring sent out across the surface, he'd laugh a gruff laugh. The laugh of a man who'd smoked non filter cigarettes his entire life and worked hard long days for the same amount of time or longer. He was at that point where it didn't matter what was playing at the end of his line. That's not what it was about.

He'd laugh at me when I'd finally hoist a pan fish out of the water and sigh, "Awww, not another one!" He'd just laugh. And now, after years and years I understand why. I've never been a fish counter or a size chaser, but still, at some point epiphanies hit you, and this young boy on the bank complaining about a pan fish below his bobber was mine.

My own two sons don't complain about a pan fish or a creek chub taking their marabou jig and running with it, they smile and laugh as the fish is lifted above the water. They're just happy to have a slimy, scaly, thrashing creature attached to that extension of themselves, their fishing rod. I'm sure at some point it'll become to them what it becomes to most of us. The quest for some huge mythical monster or the hopes of a hundred fish day. But then sooner or later, usually later, it'll come full circle.

They won't realize it at first that they're specifically casting to that greedy little bluegill, that tiny thief of a pumpkinseed, that alley way mugger of a rock bass, and having fun. But then on one such time on the water they'll realize it and wonder at what point they actually started aiming for them specifically and not worrying about that big old bass or that wary trout.

Another young high school kid complained once, "I hate those little things. They're such a pain." I wanted to tell him "Someday you'll appreciate them for what they are, someday you'll be hoping for them," but I let it go. High school kids don't listen to us anyhow, because we don't know anything. I remember.

83

"If it was easy everyone would be doing it." "That's why they call it fish'n and not catch'n." People get it, a lot of them just don't realize it until that epiphany hits. Then it's like starting all over again.

Blood Shot Fly Fishing

It's called *"Group 3."* I go to work Monday and Tuesday for the day shift, have Wednesday and Thursday off, then go in at 11:30PM Thursday night and do the same the next three nights. Monday Morning I'm back on days. It's a vicious cycle, it's no fun, and the person that came up with such a shift must be evil incarnate or just a real asshole. One of the two. Not only does it mess with your sleep schedule, but it messes with your fishing time. You wake up wondering what day it is and where you should be, or if you're missing something. And if you're me, when you get home in the morning from being up all night, the sun rise giving you your second wind, you question whether or not you should go fishing or go to bed. I may look like the walking dead...But I'll look like the walking dead in waders. I can sleep anytime. Anytime I'm not fishing.

I somehow made it through a night of greasy and smelly mechanics coveralls, foam ear plugs crammed into my ear canals, and battles with machinery that wants to chew you up and spit you out like some half-digested undercooked meat. My only weapons are wrenches and ratchets, God what I wouldn't give for a hand grenade. I made the short drive home. And I made it through getting the boys on the school bus and seeing Holly leave for work. And then my second wind, my fishing wind kicked in.

A brown rabbit strip and white faux fur streamer was the only one I carried. My 7wt in hand, my wader boots carried me down our street and I hooked left to the bridge, the Oriskany Creek passing beneath it. I was holding off sleeping to fish, but only for so long. I meant to make this a short outing, hence the single streamer. I'd either catch a couple fish or lose the streamer, at which point I'd give in to sleep. Of course, I could get skunked too. There *was* a method to my madness if you looked hard enough.

I had an idea how the fly would swim as I tied it the day before, placing the brown on top and the white underneath as the belly, my goal was to imitate the two-tone look of the small minnows in the creek. As I stepped into the creek I hung the fly in the slow water and

85

smiled as it wiggled and swam, looking like a bait fish struggling against the current.

Normally I preferred to go down stream more to get away from the bridge and the manmade scenery and into the woods, but today I wanted to stay a little closer, so I didn't have so far to walk back once my second wind died, which could be at any moment. I made a cast to the bottom of an old rough cut stone bridge piling, into a five foot square shadow at best. The water bordering it on three sides filled with sunlight, clear enough to make out every cobble stone, pebble, and old timber of the original bridge that once stood there.

The streamer landed in the shadow against the old piling with a dull slap, and I immediately began a slow jerking strip to keep it in the small dark water before the current which picked up speed as it pushed around the piling carried it away downstream. Just as the streamer cleared the shadow and made the sun light I saw it. A movement, a fish advancing out of the dark, then a mouth opened and inhaled the imposter and made its turn to go back to its ambush spot. I lifted the rod tip and set the hook.

As bronze hell broke loose I held on, the fighting butt of the 7wt pushing against my forearm. I reeled. The fish fought. First the fish tried to go down stream, finding it couldn't go any further and flanked on both sides by the old stone bridge piling walls, it turned and came straight upstream, my line going slack for a couple seconds. I stripped in slack as fast as I could until the smallmouth left the pilings and hooked right. It meant to try to escape down the next row of pilings and the line went tight again.

The game was played, the fight fought like this three times until I finally dragged the fish into shallow ankle deep water. The bass in the Oriskany Creek range in color and markings depending on the section they live in, and this one was the color of brass that had years of patina and character. I could've fished more, longer, down to at least the bottom side of the bridge, but something told me this was good enough. End on a good note, after only a couple casts. A good fish. A good battle. A fine morning. And now to bed to replay the fight in my head as I drifted off to sleep in the morning daylight, the rest of my friends at work, thinking about fishing.

Sight Fishing to Bonefish

We started the summer off with a ton of rain. This creek was blown out, high and brown more often than not, and the few days that it was fishable were singles in between weeks of non-fishable conditions. Now it's gone to the opposite extreme. The rains ceased a couple weeks ago or more and the Oriskany Creek is low and clear.

As I stand on dry cobblestone creek bed I scan the shallows. There's a deeper channel that runs about twelve feet out from me here and there, inconsistently. I believe in this deeper water is where I'll find the fish, taking refuge in what little darkness they can find. The water is so clear that in most places I can see everything as if I were looking through the glass of a fish aquarium, even as the deeper channel darkens on the bottom, I can still make out rocks and fish shapes.

After walking and silently surveying the creek I finally see the rolling of golden bronze along the bottom just downstream of a large rock. I remove the small streamer from the hook keeper of the glass rod. The sink tip line shoots through the guides without effort and with only one false cast a mixture of tan rabbit fur and natural mallard flank feathers touches down with a dull slap on the opposite side of the creek. I give it two twitches to get it into deeper water then strip it back to me. It takes four or five times, adjusting the strips first faster, then slower, longer, then shorter, then a dead drift with a slight twitch now and then. The last rewards me with the first fish of the day, a small bronze back around ten inches.

Farther downstream I find myself amazed at the crystal clear water flowing slowly before me, so low and so slow it hardly makes a sound. The sun light reflects in bright lines against the leaves above and a leaf floating along here and there are the only evidence of the waters movement. The only hues come from the green bordering and overhanging the water, the full branches giving a hint of green as the water gathers the light from all around it and absorbs the color from the dry world above it.

I move along slowly, as if I were one of the fishermen I read about in the magazines in articles about sight fishing to bone fish on salt flats or huge browns in the spectacular crystal clear rivers of Patagonia. I spot fish and freeze. I send the sink tip line rocketing through the guides of the 5wt and I'm rewarded a couple times by quick battles with silver scales and bronze brawlers. Fall fish and smallmouths.

Downstream just a bit farther the water widens and gains depth for a short stretch, the sandy bottom absorbing all the light filtered through the green foliage and creating a pocket, a space of unknown. I wade to just over my waist and as I scan the bottom out further to where I only now can make out slight shapes in the depth before nothing at all I see fish swimming to within eight or nine feet of me. They ignore the streamer and circle back and forth in agitated patterns. My presence has given them lock jaw but not sent them for cover.

It's a small streamer, no more than an inch and a half at most. I inspect the knot, I straighten rabbit fur, and I send it some thirty odd feet to the far bank and give it time to sink low as it slowly drifts downstream. This volume of dark, deep pool will bring the best of both smallmouth and big minnow, the fall fish, to me today. I see carp here more often than not but never manage to hook into one, and the local kids here in town that set up with worms and sinkers swear they're catching trout, I just nod and neither confirm nor deny my beliefs in their fish stories. Clear water. A sandy bottom. Beautiful conditions. Black vertical stripes and blotches against a greenish-bronze and silver scales compete for my memories of the day.

Just as the sight fishing of turquoise salt flats of the Keys are thousands of miles away, so in my mind is work which is merely a ten minute ride from here. So is my house which is only several hundred yards away. And so is the road on the other side of the trees, maybe fifty yards or less. The silver scales of the fall fish. I'm sight fishing to my bone fish. *Everything* is thousands of miles away.

To Be a Fishing Guide

I've been doing a lot of reading lately. Fishing stories mainly. I've been doing quite a bit of writing too. Again, fishing stories. And I've been tying a few flies. And jigs of marabou and rabbit strips for my buddies that don't fly fish. I'll suck them into this madness yet. I've found myself over the past couple years really questioning what it is I want out of life, seeing as how I'm knocking on 40yrs old and don't count on seeing 80, half way through life or more seems as good a time as any to wonder if you're doing it right. Some might call it a mid-life crisis. I don't call it anything except reality.

A couple of the books I've read recently were authored by fishing guides. Great stories of leaving promising careers and familiar surroundings behind in search of fresh air, freedom, and doing what they want to do for life. Not for a living...for life. That's not something I read word for word in any of those books. But that's what I get from it all. These men and women that pull up stakes and head out to far off states to take people fishing, they might make money, whether big or small. They're going to pay the bills if they're lucky. But they're not doing it for a living. They're doing it to live.

Yesterday I found myself going through old pictures on my phone of the past 2-3 years. Fishing pictures dominate most of the memory on my phone, followed by shots from up on the towers I used to climb for a living, which, ironically, breathed life back into something I'd always taken for granted and even pushed to the side for a few years...fishing.

Thinking about all of this, I thought for a moment. Had I really made the right decision about leaving the tower climbing job for a job at home in a giant alloy plant? A closed up, stuffy, hot, dirty factory? Maybe if I could do it all over again from when I left home, instead of going in the Air Force, I'd head out west and become a guide. Or down to South America, New Zealand, Alaska, maybe north into the Adirondacks. Another moment of thoughts had me thinking I should just close up my tool box at work one day and never open it again. Just go become a guide. Then I remembered. I'm not a good fisherman. I kind of suck at it, no matter how much I love it. Then I came across a picture on my phone that blew my mind.

It turns out, that over the past 4 or 5 years, that I've actually become a fishing guide. Rowing a canoe, pointing out the submerged logs where largemouths lie in wait for a frog or minnow. Directing where to cast, how to get the most action out of the marabou jig I tied for this outing the night before. How to cast upstream and let it drift and bounce the bottom with the current. Coaching as the fight is fought. "Wait, let it take it a little...set the hook *now!* Keep the tip up! Keep the pressure on! Don't let it go slack! It's ok, you're doing great, nice job!"

When they're ready to try the fly rod, once again I'll be ready to give the best instruction I can on the water. It doesn't bother me at all that right now they only want their spinning rods. I picked up the fly rod late in life. The fact that they want to go fishing with me at all is *all* that matters. At some point, one of them is going to set down their Zebco or their Ugly Stick and ask me to hand over my fly rod. And I will. Imagine that. I'm a fishing guide after all. The tips are better than I ever expected too.

The Big Dam Brown

Besides the whole getting *purposefully lost* thing, besides the finding my inner peace thing, and besides the whole getting outdoors thing, there's something to be said about the whole *you never know what you might find at the end of your line* thing. I think fly fishermen, more than others, seem to think that they can go out in search of a specific fish and with the right patterns zero in on that one species all day. Part of that mindset may come from fishing dry flies on trout streams, as what you're doing is giving the trout what you can already see they're eating. Sometimes.

But there's still that margin for variations in victories, like when the creek chubs are competing in the same waters for a meal. You might be disappointed that it's not the hog of a brown you thought it was, but it's a dose of reality that, just maybe, you don't know quite as much as you think you know. Close the dry fly box and open up the meat locker full of fifty shades of streamers and the confidence of guessing what's at the end of the next tug probably goes right out the window, unless you're fishing in your neighbors coy pond on a drunken dare by the light of a full moon.

This past year I'll admit to chasing more trout than anything else, but I wouldn't call myself a trout bum. I have a regular job, a house, a car payment, a wife and kids, I'd say I'm just a trout *enthusiast*.

The trout bum only makes enough money to keep fishing and keep a roof over one's head, be it a home with an overgrown lawn and dirty siding, a motel room close to this week's river, or a tent. The trout bum has no time to settle down with a family and if it does happen it was never seen coming and most likely doesn't last long.

I'm not entirely sure why I chased trout so much, other than I really like fishing rivers and streams because I have no boat for large bodies of water to chase bass, and the places I was going to hunt for the browns and brookies were nothing short of remote and beautiful. And fishing places where the dominating species is trout may have helped me to begin to fool myself into the false thinking that I too was able to pick what fish I wanted to catch, and go out and catch that very fish and nothing else. But a streamer cast in water holding a mixed bag of fish is all it takes to be snapped back to reality. No matter what you think you know, you are *not* in control.

I left the 7wt hanging on the wall for a change, even though I was going to the dam, where I knew from past experiences, and past deliberate trips to hunt specifically for pike that there were indeed northerns patrolling the white water rolling over the borders of the dam's discharge pool. I hadn't been successful. Let's not go thinking that I know what I'm doing just because I know they're there, but I did lose a couple, miss a couple, and see a couple all on different occasions at this very spot. But during a few attempts I'd also caught smallmouths and walleye as well so all bets were off.

I decided I was going there to catch a couple walleye and I rigged up the glass 5wt with a sink tip line and grabbed my streamer box. The same streamer box mind you, which I pulled from during the pike attempts, and the same streamer box that I carried with me while chasing both large and smallmouth bass. But I was walleye fishing this time. I knew what I was going to catch after all, and I knew the 5wt would be just fine.

After a bunch of casts from the concrete wall and not so much as a flash of fin or scales I waded out through the weed bed up to the face of the dam like I normally do. The wall was my normal spot for walleye, but out here I'd caught smallies and missed northerns, and even caught a largemouth once. Carp were everywhere out here as well, but if the pike were difficult for me, then the carp, I'd decided, were just all out assholes. A fish for another story, a story for another time.

So I'm not sure why I waded out there since I was after walleye, but regardless, there I was, convinced every cast held the potential for a nice marble eye and nothing else. I was casting a streamer that usually did really well in the Oriskany Creek for smallmouths, so again, why I was in this spot, fishing this fly, convinced a walleye was about to bend the rod is a little beyond me looking back, but it must have made sense at the time.

I made a cast across a fast shoot of white water that blasted out of the corner of the discharge pool, I counted to three to let the lead dumbbell eyes get it down into the turbulence a little and then stripped fast to make it appear that a baitfish was making a break for it, rushing out of the white churning stuff to haul ass across open water for cover in a panic. Now you can speculate, as all fisherman do from time to time, that a walleye would be sitting on the bottom just under the fast rough stuff waiting for a minnow to be washed out dizzy and confused, an easy meal. You can also speculate that the walleye might, for a second, study its prey and decide that this was indeed a helpless and tasty meal, but in all reality to speculate that a fish having a brain the size of a pea has much room for anything that resembles reasoning might be a far stretch. Let's speculate that a fish is hungry, it sees something dart as if to escape, and as running from a grizzly will most certainly cause it to run you down and eat you, the fish motivated by instinct gives chase and opens its mouth.

The streamer probably hadn't even cleared the white water yet and the line went tight, the rod tip danced, and I strip set the hook. The rod doubled over and the fish cut into the white water and line peeled off the old Medalist reel Holly had bought me at a garage sale years ago. My first thought was that walleye don't fight like that, once they're off the bottom they just kind of stop fighting and you haul them up like a sack full of wet socks. Maybe it was a small pike the way it was staying down deep and continuing to take line. But then I thought no, *must be a smallmouth*. It was fighting to frantic, using a lot of muscle and erratic movements. Whatever it was, it was pissed.

I hauled back on the rod and the white glass arched from a foot above the cork handle out and back down to the tip, pointing out the spot under the water where the prize fought back. For a second I thought I should ease up or lose it, but then I remembered I had on a leader of 20lb test fluorocarbon, a decision I'd made that I thought might aid me in the event that there were teeth in proximity to the streamer on some odd chance, so I doubled my pressure and decided to winch in whatever it was without much more of a hassle.

Realizing it was losing, it jumped. It jumped again, and a third time. I pulled my net off my back and after two misses scooped up the win, *not* a walleye. I'd come so sure of walleye that my mind raced at the sight, how could I be so wrong? My heart pounded, harder now that the fish was safely in the net than when I didn't know what it was. Not only was it not a walleye, but it also wasn't a bass, and also wasn't a pike. My hand slid under its body and I hefted a good weight of a gorgeous *brown.* As I waded across the weed bed to the rocks I almost tripped and fell in twice, my mind still racing and ignoring what my feet where trying to do. I don't hardly ever catch big fish, and I never measure them, because that's just not what it's about for me. That being said I knew this was my biggest trout to date and really wanted to know how long it was.

Well, hang on. I'm a fisherman, which means I know how long every fish is automatically without ever pulling a measuring tape out, and this one was well over twenty inches, but I wanted proof. The best I could do was lay the fly rod down and hold the trout next to it, then measure the rod at home to provide the proof my fishing buddies would need before believing such a story. Seemed like a solid plan at the time.

When I revived the fish I took note that this was the first one big enough to allow me to hold it just In front of its tail in the water, most were always small enough that the tail would slide right through my hand.

I almost waded back out to fish some more then thought better of It. I'd leave the walleye alone, they could buy that trout a beer later on for breaking my concentration. At home I measured the rod to where the fish's tail ended and it came out to eighteen and a half inches, so we'll call it twenty-two. But there was that nagging fact that I'd gone for walleye, so sure of them, and caught none. I was finally not chasing trout, and what did I do? I caught a trout. I wondered to myself, "No walleye...was that a win or a fail?" It's probably better not to speculate.

The Angler's Path

As I turn off the pavement the soft rumble of dirt pressed under rubber tells me I'm here. A dead end sign greets me, its faded yellow paint blends in with the fall foliage surrounding it yet its flat and metallic form stands in contrast. It tells me at the end of this dirt road there's nothing. I know it lies.

The end of trout season is nine days away, and although I swear I'm not simply just a trout hunter, that I chase any fish, I've found myself in an excited state of brookie anxiety over the past couple weeks. I have a brown trout creek running behind my house that's open to catch and release year round, but it's not a brookie stream in the Adirondacks, and I find myself thinking that, even though I've chased brookies more this year than any other in the past, I haven't chased them enough. Like the dying old man in a hospital bed who realizes in his last moments that he must make peace with his demons, I feel that I must find my peace here, now, before it's too late.

At the trail head I sit on the tailgate and kick off my boots, squirming my way into sixty dollar waders that are seeing me through the end of their second season, one more than I thought they'd make it through. They're looking rough. As I walk past the truck to begin my hike in I glance at the lock knobs to make sure I've locked the cab and catch myself in the reflection of the glass. A scruffy face and a dirty wrinkled up ball cap, I'm looking rough too. But I don't feel it. The strong smell of the pines is in the air, leaves of yellow, red and orange fall from the trees above as a cool breeze rustles them loose. I look rough, I feel content.

A mile and a half, a twenty minute hike. Anticipating the waters I'll find at the end of the path should make this walk in seem to take forever, but my anxiety has turned to patience somehow, a patient walk that would leave blue haired mall walkers in my dust. I may be walking, but my speed probably matches that of a light jog. I pass under the bright fall foliage. I leave the path to skirt around fallen trees, and I travel through dark tunnels of evergreens that close in narrow and low as if to try to keep me on the straight path to the trout

I come to hunt. At last I hear the sound of water crashing, and the end of the path comes into view. Where the path ends, the true path begins.

Water rushes and smashes over rock, and it seems that our one and only rain over this entire summer two days ago has brought the stream up a good two feet. What's been a low and trickling stream full of slow pools and clear tea colored flowing water now looks angry, a mix of mostly white water with pockets of dark red behind the largest boulders. I realize that I most likely have nothing heavy enough to get down to the fish holding in the deep pockets on the bottom fast enough. It doesn't bother me in the least. I'll travel upstream anyhow. I'll follow the path of water back to the truck.

Along the way I've got plenty of time to think, something I normally don't do much of while fishing. Normally it's me and the fish, and my thoughts keep to themselves unless they're thoughts of where should I cast, what fly should I use, and where the hell did that tree come from behind me that my leader's now tangled in.

But this trip is different. I think of how I came to having this fly rod in my hand. I think of the beginnings, a young boy, a Zebco, a worm and a bobber. I think of my Grandfather casting an Eagle Claw bait hook with a worm dug from his small green pepper garden in Utica into a small water fall and pulling out a trout. I remember my frustration as I attempted to do the same and came up with nothing time and time again, as my Grandfather laughed at my scowls and unhooked another. He knew I'd get it someday, that must have been the joke. The fact that I'm driving almost eighty miles to wander a stream trying to outsmart a six inch fish with a brain smaller than the size of the tip of my pinky finger is the punchline. I'm just now getting it, thirty something years later.

I only find three pools large enough to give my streamer enough time to get down deep, down to the fishes level. Over a couple hours wandering along the rapid flowing stream I manage to find three fishable pools, and I see three flashes and slashes of coppery orange bellies, and I miss all three of them.

Getting back to the truck, as I'm sitting on the tailgate tugging at my worn out waders, I realize this is the first time I've been skunked on this stream. It doesn't bother me, but I find it ironic that my thoughts had carried me back to my earliest memories of trout fishing, and hauling in a worm on a hook and nothing more time after time. Skunked. I'd been struggling with my place in life for the better part of the past year, trying to figure out where I was and where I'm going.

Just like the dead end sign and this path that waited at the end of the dirt road, and the first time I found it. You don't know where your path leads until you get there. This particular trail is a path that leads you in a circle. You begin and end here, on the tailgate, tugging at waders. I thought about my Grandfather laughing as I frowned at my fishless hook. Sometimes the path that simply returns you to the beginning is the right one.

Wannabe Trout Bum Misadventures

I met JP at his place right after the midnight shift on a Wednesday morning. There were only a couple weeks left and we only had a half a day free before we each had to meet work and family obligations, so we were heading for a place JP had found on the maps, not far away, a river we'd both fished numerous times, but never in the area he pointed to on the GPS screen on the Jeep's dash. The idea, one only a couple trout bums could come up with was to use half a day near the end of this trout season to scout out water to fish next season. Scouting I decided was a safe way of saying "We'll take our fly rods and check this place out, but if we don't catch anything it's OK...We're just scouting." Fishermen aren't just liars, we unconsciously invent excuses ahead of time for numerous scenarios. We're just that good.

We parked in a small clearing on the side of a dirt road with a state camp site tag nailed to a tree about thirty minutes from home. As we pulled in I was thinking I didn't know I could find brookies this close to home. This could be a cool spot. The GPS map showed the river only about a thousand yards from the road so we threw on rain jackets and slung rod tubes over our shoulders. It hadn't rained all summer, and now the weather man and the radar both agreed that the wet stuff was finally on the way. We needed the rain badly. Not only were all the water levels down dangerously low, but as of the day before there was actually a wild fire burning in the Adirondacks! Not thousands of acres like you see out west, but about a hundred, still something simply unheard of in this corner of the country anymore.

We expected to find a river that was really low from the drought and wanted nothing more than the waters to get back up to their normal levels. We just didn't want it to happen during our half of the day. JP pulled out some nifty satellite compass looking thing from his pocket, pushed a button, nodded, and assured me that it had just marked the spot where we stood at the Jeep and that later on our return from the river, should we need it, it would lead us right back. But it was only a thousand yards or so, give or take. We probably wouldn't need it. Into the woods we went, in search of wild Trout.

A GPS map that shows you grey lines that are roads, blue lines that are rivers, and fills the rest in with green that's everything else that's not a road or a river shows you just enough to give you ideas. The ideas being *if I stand here, point that direction and walk, I'll run right into what I'm aiming at.* What such a simple map doesn't show you is everything else. Elevation changes. Ridges. Gullies. Slopes and Hills. But all you have to do is walk straight across all these things. Just walk straight, and you'll end up right where you want to be. Unless you come upon a dry stream bed that doesn't show up on such a simple map and throw out the whole walking straight thing because you figure *this obviously drains into the river and it's a lot easier to follow than traipsing through the dense undergrowth, climbing ridges and hills and across gullies. Let's just follow this.* It seemed like a good plan at the time.

After leaving an arrow on the ground formed from a couple river birch branches to show us on our way back where to leave the streambed, we made our way along a grassy, waterless drainage, hopping over moss covered rotting tree trunks and dry cobble stones that sat there like turtles in their shells, the drought giving us an easy path to follow. The problem with easy is it also means faster. And the problem with faster is when you're moving in the wrong direction fast, you get farther off course in a shorter amount of time. After getting the feeling that we were now moving away from the river and that we should have found it already and contemplating back tracking, I decided I could hear the sound of water moving over rocks. In a few more yards the streambed we were in intersected with another that traveled to our left and downhill at a much more aggressive grade toward the sound of the water.

At the river we found what we'd expected. What would've normally been about forty feet of water was about twenty feet of shallow water and twenty feet of dry riverbed half of which was sun bleached cobble stones and the other half tall grass, both of which should have been under water. There was however a change to a slow pool that spanned almost the whole width downstream about a hundred yards so we made our way to it, slipping and stumbling our way across the damp and shaded round rocks and boulders of the sadly low flowing river.

At the pool we strung up our rods. JP tied on a dry fly. Myself, being a horrible dry fly fisherman, tied on a small streamer and made my way out onto a large boulder above the head of the pool. On my second cast stripping back across the pool I got the telltale rapid fire hit of a small brookie. As I lifted the rod tip I turned to JP and smiled. "They're here." Only to have the streamer pop from the water and land near his feet. After a few more casts and nothing I gave up the spot to JP and he drifted the dry fly a few times and came up empty.

Content that we'd found the river and at least gotten a bite, and knowing in the backs of our minds that we had a time limit and the way in hadn't been as quick and straight forward as we planned we broke down our rods and started back up the river side, slipping and fumbling clumsily about the rocks once again. JP muttered something about walking on greased bowling balls and I chuckled.

Back up the streambed we once again made our way over rotting trees and moss covered rocks. We could've left this one and traveled back up the first to find the river birch arrow, but at some point most likely distracted by working around a downed tree or something we must have passed it and kept going.

We stopped. It wasn't raining yet, so instead of keeping the rain off us from the outside, we were sweating and getting soaked inside the jackets. But mosquitos hovered so we kept them on. JP pulled out the nifty satellite deal and handed it to me since I was in front. I held it in my hand and watched the digital arrow that was supposed to point to the Jeep slowly rotate back and forth, searching, but not finding. I remembered the satellite radio stations and how they'd cut in and out in the trucks when I worked on the road. Mountains, hills, buildings and bridges, even heavy tree cover would block the satellites and a good song would suddenly go dead. The arrow continued to point back and forth unable to make a decision for us. "Yea, this isn't going to work out to well for us." I handed it back.

Next up cell phones emerged from pockets and I smiled to find that we actually had great coverage. For a few seconds I was proud to have been a cell tower climber for a few years, knowing it was guys like me, and my buddies still up there on the towers that were the reason at this very moment we could pull up a map in the palm of our hand that would show us our location and get us back to the road.

To make a long story short, once we wandered for about another twenty minutes we finally figured out which direction we needed to move in, but our confidence didn't fully return until we saw the break in the trees ahead that meant we'd made it back to the dirt road. By the time we were peeling off rain jackets soaked in sweat back at the Jeep we figured out that we'd come back out to the road a half mile away from the parking spot. But looking at the map now, we hiked at least double the distance a combination of north and east.

As rubber mud treads contacted black top five minutes later rain drops began to smack the windshield. JP turned and asked with a sarcastic grin "So, want to do that again?" There may have been some disappointment buried in the question, the sting of no fish and of getting just a little lost in the woods. "I think it's this way, what do *you* think?" The question had been repeated by us both several times out there. I replayed it over in my head. Did I want to do it again...? Does a dog actually learn from getting sprayed by a skunk or does he get sprayed again because he's a dog and *dogs chase skunks*?

Walleye

You know how it is. You just don't always have the time to drive to someplace out of the way and secluded from the manmade world. At least I don't. I've got to be to work at 11:30 at night, so lately, now that I can't chase brook trout in the Adirondacks anymore because the season is over until April, and now that the creek out back's gotten slow with the drop in temperatures, I've found myself coming home from work in the mornings, putting the boys on the bus, kissing the wife good bye as she goes out the door to work, and then vacuuming and doing the dishes. Yea... right. The boys get on the bus, the wife goes to work, and I jump into my waders. I point the truck at the Delta Lake dam, one of the spots close enough to home to not need to load up the canoe and still be able to chase the elusive northern pike I've been trying for all year.

A lesser angler would've given up at this point with as many follows, missed strikes, break offs, and set hooks that *just came out* as I've had. But when my wife tells me I'm stubborn, she's right. In this instance it's working to my advantage, because I haven't figured out how to give up on the idea yet.

I may have spent 3 million dollars on different set ups and so many various fly patterns that I've spent countless hours under a light in the corner of a dark room tying, but eventually, hopefully before the 5 million dollar mark, I'll put a pike in my net. Sink tips. Steel leaders of every type out there, none of which I like to use. Heavy fluorocarbon leaders. Heavy mono. Packs of hooks and then more packs of hooks. More buck tails, more flash, more marabou, more wire for articulated streamers. More dumbbell eyes. A full sinking line, maybe some holographic eyes, maybe a different color hackle. More flash still and more hooks... maybe a twenty-five dollar T-bone steak for a trailer will do the trick. Or maybe I should just buy some beer, go sit by the water's edge and see if I can't figure out if it's a pale ale or a porter that they want. I'm running out of ideas...but my patience hangs on.

So at the dam I wade under an old decrepit bridge and up the side of a weed bed, casting well in front of me, stripping streamers along the edge searching for that toothy missile I know is waiting in ambush out

103

there somewhere. I've had them strike and break off too small of a leader. I've had them follow close enough so that I had no more line to strip in and had to keep it moving with the tip of the rod only to have them turn and swim away. Had them strike only to rip the streamer away to soon in my excitement, and had them take it, peel line of the reel, and in the excitement and fear of a break off never set the hook only to have them just *let go*. I've got a semi-permanent hand imprint on my forehead from that one that I'm hoping is gone before Christmas. Those would make for interesting pictures in the years to come.

On this day I get none of the above working the weeds. Once I'm close enough to the dam's discharge pool where the water cascades down a cement slope and churns white and frothy as it becomes the river I turn my casts to the white turbulence itself. Pike and walleye will hold right at the base of the cement pool walls, under and just behind the churning mess and strike out at food being tossed around. I send a red and white 4 inch streamer into the chaos and let it get sucked down underneath. Nothing.

I push my way through the weed bed. It's like trying to wade through a can of spinach the size of an above ground pool, about waste deep and so dense you have no idea of what your next step will find. In the summer I worry about snapping turtles, it's a spot that I don't care if it's a hundred degrees, I'm *not* wet wading. Its waders or I'm just not going out there. Not that waders would stop a snapping turtle from taking a chunk out of calf, but it makes me feel braver anyhow.

The last time I was here it was carp that freaked me out. I'm pushing through the weeds, and I keep hearing this sucking sound. It wasn't until the third stop and look around that I spotted the carp face just poking out of the green five feet away, and then, knowing what I was looking for, I realized there must have been half a dozen of them within twenty feet of me, all busy in the task of making the sucking sound, taking something from the top side of the weed bed, what, I don't know. Bugs, algae, snails, something. I couldn't catch one on the fly rod in such a horrible mess of cabbage, but I'll bet if I'd tried I

104

could've grabbed one with my hands. I'll bet there's also a good chance that the sucking sound they were making was merely their way of saying I sucked. Carp can be real jerks, but that's another story for another time.

I make my way through and back out to open water, a good fifty feet of it between me and the dam, and I fail here as well to attract the attention of anything. Feathers and flash may as well be an empty tippet with nothing on it for what it's worth today. I turn around and push back through the weeds to return to dry land.

Before I leave I decide I should walk the wall around to the discharge pool, a spot where you can look down on the white tumbling and churning mess from about fifteen feet above. It's a hard spot to fly fish because you're so much higher than the water, but from up here I've seen good pike shoot from the discharge's white water to devour a Rapala or two when I used to fish a spinning rod here. My 7wt launches the red and white streamer through the air and it drops about fifty feet out, disappears on the edge of the white and I can barely make it out as it's carried out and away, a white flutter and flash now and then to show me where it is. After three or four casts I open my streamer box and choose a brown and olive streamer.

As I finish tying It on something small and dark in the white water catches my eye. Is that leaves being churned up from the bottom? That makes no sense in my head so I stand and watch. There they are again, about four to six inches, dark brown and tapered shapes emerging in the turbulence, seeming to fight to stay in place, then they're gone again. Fish. Some kind of small brown fish is hiding in the roughest water it can find. I have to assume there's something underneath pushing them up into hostile water, and I'm fairly sure, once again from my spinning rod trips here, that it's walleye. No sooner do I paint the picture in my head, I see a dark, much larger fish shape come up to the top of an eddy just downstream, it splashes at the surface and rolls on its side to return to the bottom. A walleye, there's no doubt in my mind.

It occurs to me, I'm now spot fishing for walleye the way one would for trout, watching them rise for food being carried by a current, and

105

I've unknowingly just tied on a streamer that matches the hatch. This is too good to be true. After figuring out the cast and the drift to get it to the fish I start catching. Most are in the 13 to 15 inch range as far as I can tell without measuring them. But there's one, the one I saw splash at the surface that I can't get to take my fake. I watch the fish come off the bottom and swirl at the feathers and flash several times. It's not moving on, not getting spooked, but it's not falling for my game either. I make a final cast and let the white smashing current take it to the bottom and sweep it out, and I begin reeling in to go home.

Six Walleye is good enough, the last proves smarter than the rest and I'm prepared to leave him be. Then as I reel in, the line goes tight. It's much heavier that the others. Walleye aren't known as super hard fighters, but this one is more like trying to lift a rock off the bottom, it must be bigger. It fights to stay on the bottom but I'm rigged up with a 20lb test leader for pike, so I don't worry about a break off and put a good arch in the rod as I pry it from the bottom. Once it starts up, it's like any other walleye, like a child that goes limp as the parent scolds it and holds it by the arms trying to force it to walk to its room, the Walleye just gives up the fight and forces me to carry its weight to the net.

It's a fine fish, not the biggest marble eye I've ever caught, but it's twenty-two inches. I measure this one. And it's fat, much bigger than the others. It occurs to me on my walk to the truck that no, I haven't landed my pike yet, but a walleye has teeth, and my streamer looks ragged from all the teeth that gnawed on it in the last forty minutes. Close enough for today, and it's another species checked off the list on the fly.

I spot fished to walleye, matched the hatch, and caught seven. Seven's supposed to be a lucky number, so this is truly one of those times when I'll admit that some days it's better to be lucky than good. But I did match the hatch, so, maybe I was good. But if I was good then I have standards to try to live up to each time I go out, and that'll never last. I'm going with lucky. Yea, lucky *is* good.

Time, Money, and Fly Fishing

Two weeks. It'd been two weeks since I'd been fishing. Two weeks is a long time for someone that sometimes fishes every day. Painful. Agonizing. The last time I'd been out was the final float of the year on JP's flat bottom boat with him and his wife Bobbi Jo, a short outing on Lake Delta. We skimmed water sometimes only inches deep, possible only because of the jet drive. It may not make the power a prop does, but it gains you clearance enough to keep cruising on without lifting the motor from the water in super shallow conditions.

As we cruised out to super skinny water I saw the look of horror on a kayaker's face as he was certain we were going to come to a sudden halt, bodies flying through the air like rag dolls. We only had to raise the motor out and push pole ahead with the sound of scraping rocks below our feet once. Back into deeper water we cast to rolling carp and searched for signs of life along weed beds. We trailered the boat one last time for 2015 without hooking a single fish, but it could have been much worse. Some people *were working* you know.

Two weeks. Since that day two weeks had gone by and I found my daily life too hectic to get on any water. Pretty depressing seeing as I can walk to the creek out back in about 2 minutes. I had no idea why I couldn't make it work, but I remember thinking the first week "I'll make up for it next week." Then the next week saw contractors tearing the electric base board heat out of our house and racing to replace it with a new hot water system before winter weather showed its ugly face any day now. I stuck around the house, staying out of the way in my tying and writing room, switching back and forth between the two activities, breaking them up now and then with a YouTube video selection of someone in a warm and tropical place casting flies to exotic salt water fish.

All the while the thought of the irony, how installing this new heating system was going to save money in the long run yet it would be sucking money out of the bank account now that couldn't be spent on fishing related wants and needs. I told myself I needed a spare spool for my 7wt reel, a sink tip line to go on that spool, and a new pair of waders that I wouldn't *need* until spring but felt the *need* to buy now.

107

I think most die-hard fisherman when it comes down to it would be content to live off of Ramen Noodles and grilled cheese sandwiches if it meant the bulk of their paycheck could go to fishing necessities. Necessities of course are anything from new rods and reels all the way down to a deck of playing cards with trout on them and anything in between. It can be a little vague sometimes as to what's really necessary in the mind of a fly fishing fanatic. But being a fanatic has its advantages to be sure.

Aside from unlocking the secret to life, some people look at you like you might be a little crazy, a little out in left field. A good friend told me he thought I was a little deranged once while on the subject. I know he was just busting balls, but deep inside I did wonder a little if this non-fly fishing person might be even just a *little* serious. Which is fine by me. They tend to look at you a little differently than others, to not take you very seriously, which can definitely be your saving grace. Being undependable and less than "stable" can save you a lot of grief. People tend to expect less out of you, which gains you fishing time and takes the pressure off all at once.

Towards the end of the second week I was finding myself sitting on the couch in my room at 9am cradling a fly rod and replacing my coffee mug with a beer bottle, the lack of fishing and absence of any new fishing related purchases was obviously beginning to affect me.

On Thursday morning I found myself standing at the kitchen sink washing a cereal bowl that I'd just removed from the top rack of the dishwasher. The appliance had once again failed at its only task, to provide clean dishes. I shook my head in disgust as I scrubbed at the small specks of macaroni and cheese residue, staring out the window as Holly's conversation with me turned from the need to buy the boys some new clothes to the need to buy a new dishwasher. My head shook in disgust, partially because I had a clear view through the now naked trees out back to the creek flowing so close that you could hear it. But also partially because I was washing a bowl that had just been washed, and partially because the conversation had gone from talking about buying clothes for the boys to buying a new dishwasher, while the new heating system that would take the next fifteen years to pay off was being installed all around us.

"Well, I don't think we need to spend more than four-hundred to get what I *really* want" were the last words out of her mouth. I sighed, closed my eyes and tilted my head back. "*Fine*" I said. "Let's just spend *all* of our money on stuff that has *nothing* to do with fishing." I heard one of the heating guys chuckle in the living room as a beer called my name from the bottom drawer of the fridge.

4am Salt Dreams

I open my eyes but they refuse to focus. It's dark. Where am I? I've got a sore neck and my head is pounding like someone's put a stereo speaker in a metal fifty-five gallon drum, put the top on, and cranked the volume knob all the way up on some Iron Maiden. My eyes begin to clear up and I spot the clock on the cable box across the room on the TV stand. 3:30. Should I be at work? I lie there and think for a moment, panic trying to creep its way in, but I suppress it. No, for the past five weeks I've been working the midnight shift over the weekend but this one I finally got off somehow. I'm right where I should be. Well, almost. I'm on the couch, my bed is down the hall, but Holly must have thought I looked comfortable here...Or she's just used to having the bed all to herself.

I grab a bottle of Tylenol out of a cupboard and wash pills down with water straight out of the faucet like a kid drinking from a garden hose. Do kids even do that anymore? Whatever, my mind is still wandering just coming out of a dead sleep, but I know I'm not going back to sleep so it settles on its cruise control setting. Fly Fishing. I could flip on the boob tube and scan eight-hundred channels of nothing but reality TV crap but instead it's out to the room. I sit at the tying bench in the corner and survey the chaos of last night's tying session. Do I clean up first or pick up where I left off? I push aside bags and plumes of feathers and find the small bag of streamer hooks buried below them and tighten a hook in the vice. I haven't cast a fly rod on water in 2016, and now it's January 30th. I'm a sorry excuse for a diehard so far this year, but turning forty has had me visiting doctors, laying on tables for unpleasant procedures, and eating pain meds like candy.

I could use that as my excuse, but I still feel deep down inside like a slacker. I try to make up for it writing about fishing and tying flies, but it only lasts so long before you realize you just need to be standing in waders with a rod in your hand, *not* being a slacker.

Most winters I sit at the tying bench and tie whatever I feel like just to pass the time. I tie all year so it's not like if I don't buckle down and focus that come spring I won't have anything, it's just a constructive way to stay the course, to keep fly fishing active on the front. I might tie streamers, I might tie nymphs, and I might even tie some dries even though I'm not a huge dry fly fisherman. I just tie to stay active. I tie whatever I feel like at the moment. This winter is different. In March we'll be taking the kids to Florida, a trip Holly makes each winter with the boys, one I haven't been on in six years. But this year, somehow we've worked it so that I'm going too. It's a family vacation, but my wife being the awesome, loving wife that she is has given me one day to myself for fishing, plus two early mornings before we take off for the day are mine too as long as I can get out of bed. I think I'll manage that.

I'm half way through tying a squid pattern when a roaring sound forces its way through the walls and windows. I question the presence of a slow, low flying jet at this hour since my mind was just picturing stepping off the plane into the warm Florida air. Then the yellow light strobes past the windows flashing amber across the interior of the house at split second intervals and reality checks in. Snow plow.

Here I sit in my own world dreaming of standing in thigh deep turquoise salt water, my 7wt pointed out at the horizon as line shoots through the guides. The dream shattered by a steel behemoth with a steaming cup of coffee resting in the cup holder as a driver peers through the windshield over a tall yellow steel blade. The blade scrapes ice and snow from blacktop just as it scrapes the scene from my head. It's gone, interrupting others dreams up the street and I'm once again left to my 4am day dreams.

The squid looks awesome. I'm truly happy with it as I place a drop of super glue over the thread wraps at the eye. Will it catch a fish? I don't know, but I think it looks salty for what it's worth, and it doesn't need to catch a fish here at the vice. This morning all it needs to do is make me forget about the snow plow as it makes another pass by the house hitting the opposite side of the street. It doesn't bother me nearly as much on its second pass. My eyes are studying the little squid in my vice and picturing it slowly sinking and moving along pulsing with each wave as a fish of some unrecognized salt water species makes a hard charge for a meal. My line goes tight. I strip set hard making it a point not to set the hook as if I were trout fishing back home, my feet slowly sinking

111

in the grainy white sand with each passing wave.

Cuba and Flat Billed Trucker Hats

For the past couple months now I haven't been able to pick up a fishing magazine without finding an article inside about fly fishing the flats in Cuba. Like flat billed trucker hats giving anglers street credit on the river, Cuba seems to be the next big thing in flats fly fishing. All these years I thought it was the cigars we wanted. Who knew?

Now maybe I'm just a little jealous because I'm 99% sure I'll never experience it. Or maybe it's that I can see the writing on the wall. A place that was cut off from us, untouchable, making it even more desirable, is in store for a world of change in my eyes. Once the embargo is lifted it's going to be an extreme fast forward from 1959 to the present. The streets, stuck in a time warp filled with old American cars will become modern, many of the cars scooped up by collectors or becoming parts sold and shipped off in boxes. The crumbling ancient architecture will be replaced by new high rise hotels losing all the old world charm, and tourists will flock to the country turning it into just another destination filled with t-shirt vendors and selfie sticks.

But the magazines are doing a wonderful job of selling it as the greatest flats destination on the planet, simply because you couldn't do it before, and because they want to be able to say "We were there and told you it was great when it still was, before we wrote this article about how it has now been oversold and ruined. But still, I'm like everyone else, I'd love to check it out while it's still a little harder to hire a guide than simply typing it into the Google search bar. So to deflect the obvious fact that it'll never happen, I try to counter their all-knowing editorial expertise found on their smooth and shiny pages.

They're like *"Best Flats fishing in the world!"*

I'm like "It's hot here now, and the creek out back is only knee deep or less in some places and crystal clear. If I tip my head so that the bill of my hat blocks out the trees on the other side it's just like looking at a flat."

They're like *"Bone fish, permit, and tarpon!"*

I'm like "There's suckers, creek chubs, and fall fish in the creek. They're

113

bottom feeders just like bone fish. Hell, the fall fish even has big ol' silver scales and I can sight fish to them in these clear low conditions, blocking the view of the trees with the bill of my hat.
This is just as good as Cuba."

They're like *"Hemingway's home!"*

I'm like, with a sigh not quite admitting defeat, "Well, everyone has to live *somewhere."*

They're like *"It's a warm, tropical place, with sprawling clear turquoise and white salt flats and guides poling you to the fish in the old ways in a wooden boat. Knowledge and determination mixed with a smidge of hope take the place of the cold and lifeless GPS to find your dream fish."*

I'm like "Fine. Screw you. You win."

There's always that slim chance that I could get there before it's all something totally different, I could probably scrape enough money out of our bank accounts to make the trip, but scrape would be the key word. And after the last penny was picked up off the floor in my 6yr olds room from out of the carnage of the shattered green ceramic dinosaur bank, I'd have to wait for little league season to come to an end and then quit my job for the time to make the trip. At least *one* of those is likely to happen.

Hemingway had his Cuban home when he penned "The Old Man and the Sea" and I can't hold that against him. I guess I have my little fly fishing "man cave" as everyone seems to refer to it, with a view of the creek out back, presently just shimmers of light through the fully green trees of summer now blocking my view. I suppose, circumstances what they are, that I'll have to write my masterpiece using the inspiration I have at hand, although I don't know that a book about an Upstate New York guy fighting a creek chub for three days in a skinny creek through the center of town will have quite the powerful meaning behind it. But who knows, it could gain one of those cult followings. Damn you Cuba.

Signs

A two hour wait in line for a rental car we'd reserved and paid for a month ago. A forty minute drive to the hotel. We checked in close to midnight. Standing on our balcony I knew the beach was right there. I could hear the waves. I could smell the ocean. The longer I stood there peering into the blackness, the more my eyes adjusted, until I wasn't just trying to convince myself that I could see the waves breaking just off the beach, I really could. I set an alarm for 6:30am and hit the pillow. I woke up at 5:30, stared at the ceiling for ten minutes, then got dressed and quietly gathered my rod tube and pack and headed out the door.

The sign hit me like a slap in the face, or maybe more like a sucker punch to the gut. It stood there like a century, announcing there'd be no fun to be had here. You could swim, you could sun bath, you could throw a Frisbee or a football, kick around a soccer ball, build a sand castle, fly a damn kite. But the handful of red circles with slashes through them taking up the bottom half of the sign, one contained the image of a fish and a hook. That was the knife through the heart. You've *got to be* kidding me. A freaking public beach, and no fishing.

I made my way south to the jetties I'd seen on the Google Earth images, the manmade rock walls I'd been planning on fishing for the past month. More signs. "No Trespassing. Rocks may be dangerous." You've *got to be* freaking kidding me.

The manmade sea wall went out about two-hundred feet, and where it connected to the shore line the rocks continued on down the shore in an effort to keep the ocean from over taking a new parking garage. If I made my way up to a side walk and a small patio on the side of the parking garage, then down a walk way that split between the garage and the shore, I could step down onto the rocks. I didn't see any signs from there. It seemed to me that the signs were pertaining to the jetties, not the shore. It was sketchy, I was reaching I knew.

It looked to me that if I kept my back cast low enough I wouldn't smack the wall of the second level of the garage, and if I kept it high enough, I could sneak it over the top of the chain link fence that kept the bottom level secure. Basically I had about three feet of empty space behind me at a very specific height. It was still dark, but the lights of the parking garage reached out just far enough to give a glow to the waves that sporadically crashed onto the rocks and sent sea spray into the air. I figured my best bet would be something dark with a lot of flash. I tied on a black streamer, stepped down onto the rocks from the concrete and made my first cast.

For about fifteen minutes I stood there and made cast after cast, threading the needle perfectly over the top of the chain link fence but under the floor of the next level just above it, and I didn't even snag the roof rack of the SUV on the other side of the fence. My casting was right on point that morning. In the dark, I was feeling the cast more than anything else, *almost* like I knew what I was doing. I wish I could say I grabbed a good snook off the shore line, but there's no happy ending to this story. I didn't catch squat.

Some days that's just how it is. You walk back to the hotel, take the kids down to a crappy continental breakfast, then spend the day watching their lips turn purple then blue because they won't get out of the water, and spend way too much money on cheesy souvenirs made in Taiwan in the tourist shops. The whole time everything around you is covered in fish themes...just rubbing it in. You remind yourself, this is a family vacation, not a fishing trip. It doesn't make it any less painful. I walked around the next two days with Tesla's rendition of "Signs" stuck in my head, and a fly rod tube in the back of the rental car. *Just in case*.

I'm a Horrible Dry Fly Fisherman

I don't know why, but for some reason I always thought things would get easier as you get older. You know, the longer you do something the easier it should get. The longer my boys play baseball, the better they get. The longer you're at your job, the easier it gets. You start off shaky and unconfident as a teenager behind the wheel, but the longer you drive the easier it becomes. So my question is after 40 years why is it becoming *harder* to find time to go fishing? The logic I just laid out dictates that it should be as easy as turning on a coffee pot at this point in life. But then again last week I "brewed up" a cup of hot chocolate in the Keurig and added two spoons of sugar thinking it was coffee to take to work. So that blows that theory right out the window. And in case you're wondering, hot chocolate *does not* need any more sugar.

It had been about fifteen days since I'd been fishing, and it didn't help that sixteen days earlier I'd caught a very nice and very large brook trout. My biggest ever actually. So after more than two weeks without fishing after catching a really good fish I was jonesing for the cast and the strip pretty hard. I spent the better part of a slow midnight shift scrolling across Google Earth on my phone, scanning satellite images north to south, east to west, zooming in and zooming out. I had to go *someplace* the next morning, I couldn't wait any longer. I kept coming back to this tree filled pond on a flood plain that connected to the Mohawk River when waters rose over the banks. I decided the next morning I had to go. The next morning about an hour after pulling in the driveway... I found myself with a shovel and a pile of dirt in the front yard instead. If there were any fish in that pond, they were safe from me.

Emails had been flying the previous week about fishing the following day, the morning of the 4th of July, so I still had that. After one more midnight shift of course. So after yet another, even slower and *more* boring shift sitting in a quiet and shut down production plant babysitting the place, making sure nothing leaked and flooded or sparked and burned I found myself staring at the steering wheel of the Jeep in the parking lot, my time card still smoking from swiping out. A long boring night does almost the same as a busy hard night, it makes

117

your eyelids heavy. I wondered if I should just skip the twenty-five minute drive that was going to get me a couple hours fishing and just go home and take a nap for a little bit. *Then I came to my senses*. The motor turned over, AC/DC cracked through sixteen year old door speakers and rubber rolled forward. About half way into the drive I thought to myself "You *idiot*. It's your own fault that it's so hard to get on the water these days. You *let* it happen." It may be a little more complicated than that but for the most part, yea, it's my own fault. I've gotten lazy with excuses.

Other than where I was parking I didn't know where I was going. When I pulled to the side of the narrow country road under the shade of ancient hardwoods there was JP waiting for me by a red livestock gate talking to another friend who lived down the road. They talked fishing and some politics, we weren't on the water so politics were *ok*, and Bill's blue healer came over and said hello while I struggled into my waders. We said our good byes and left the politics outside the gate as we started our walk to the river. We walked across a cow pasture on a well beaten path used probably hundreds of times a year, cows looking on chewing the cud and flipping ears and tails at bothersome flies.

I was surprised there wasn't a posted sign in sight and as we walked and talked I couldn't help but think that if we were out west somewhere doing this we'd probably have been stopped at the gate by a land owner either telling us to get lost or holding their hand out for a good chunk of my paycheck for permission to cross the land to get to public water. JP said this land owner just let anglers come and go as long as everyone was polite and left nothing behind. My faith in NY got a quick and quiet lift right then.

JP said Caddis Flies were all over the river and fish were rising, and he'd already caught a pretty nice brown. John, Mitch, and Smitty were on the water as we spoke. It all sounded great to me but it didn't leave me with much hope. I fish streamers ninety-nine percent of the time. I'm a horrible dry fly fisherman. And I'd never fished this section of river before with any success. I'd never been to this exact spot but that hardly mattered to me, I was set up for a beautiful morning of failure in my mind. But on a river, to me even failure feels *not so bad*.

This section of river was at an island and we crossed our side of the split to get to the far side of the island where I could see Smitty now. He was upstream, waist deep, and an orange fly line formed perfect loops in the air. Mitch and John were somewhere upstream above the split. If I cared about how I looked with a fly line in the air this would've been the place to care, these guys were all wonderful fly fisherman, casting instructors, guides, and rod builders. Me, I just stunk at dry fly fishing. My method of dealing with less than great casting ability has always been to make a lot of them. Sooner or later out of hundreds of bad casts you're bound to hook one fish at least out of luck if nothing else. I switched out my Medalist with the sink tip line for another reel with a floating line and JP pointed out the large caddis bouncing and fluttering on the surface out on the current. I tied on an Elk Hair that we thought matched the size about right.

As I planned my first cast a fish rose, straight out from me, then another up by Smitty, and I braced myself for frustration. The fish were rising *just* into a slower current where quarter sized foam dots spotted the surface. Between me and that slower current was a faster current which meant of course that I'd have to mend my line to keep the faster current from dragging the fly across the slower stuff. Did I mention I'm a horrible dry fly fisherman? I considered just tying on a streamer but fought off the urge and began to cast. I struggled. I made a lot of casts to make up for the quality.

The fish were rising hard now, violent takes that showed trout backs rolling and sometimes they breached and slapped down on their sides like a killer whale in an aquarium show, and while one fish kept at it up by Smitty another continuously taunted me straight out about thirty-five feet. My drifts weren't good, my mends screwed up the drifts even more and after about twenty minutes of this I tied on a streamer and continued to fail my own way. John had showed up and waded out just above me and we both agreed, at least when you don't catch anything with a streamer all the casting and stripping makes you feel like you're doing something besides watching.

I looked up stream finally to see Smitty with a bent rod. From where

119

I was it looked like a good fish, and I almost went over to see it but stopped and thought how cool it would be to have a double hook up so I kept casting. I didn't hook a fish. The trout kept jumping in front of me. I think he was laughing at me. I'm pretty sure of it.

Smitty asked John and I if we had any La Fontaines. I answered with a bit of a laugh, *"Do you really think it's going to matter in my case?"* i heard laughter from the bank. He said most definitely. It's the go to fly on this river. Well, he guides it, he should know. So he gave John and I each these little tiny hooks with six or seven deer hairs on each one over a tiny bit of dubbing that trailed off the back end like the shuck of an emerger and we stood there and almost got caught up in small talk of who knows what, when that damn fish jumped again, and I mean *jumped*. I swear I heard it yell cannon ball. JP looked at John and me and said "Will someone please go get that fish?" I laughed and as I started to wade back to my spot I sarcastically said "Yea, sure. I'm going to go *get that fish* now."

I knew I still couldn't manage my line properly for more than five or six feet before the second current and my pathetic mending miffed up the whole thing, so I changed my position. Kind of like bowling where you move over a couple boards to account for your curve, I moved upstream about five feet hoping it would be enough to get my short lived decent drift over the right spot. I made three more casts and they seemed to drift at the right speed, over the right spot. Now I just needed the right dumb trout to make the wrong move.

Boom! The fly disappeared in a ruckus of orange and tail fin and I lifted my 5wt. The line went tight. JP came down to see it as it took a little line off my reel and I palmed it, I'd never had to do that for a trout before. It stayed out in the current but I was gaining and you could see the fish clearly, it thrashed and swam circles, fighting against this unreasonably strong bug. Smitty grabbed my net and when it finally met the trout the fish didn't totally fit. There were oohs and ahhs, and I thought it was a pretty nice catch. These guys all seemed more excited than me. John measured it fast for me while I kept it wet and JP took a couple pictures.

Later on driving home it would finally hit me that what had happened was I'd caught my biggest trout ever on some tiny little hook. In the end I released a 21" brown and called it a day. I wasn't going to top that and a couple guys had to leave anyhow.

John said after I caught the only brook trout on opening day out of him and JP and myself, and after the huge brookie I caught sixteen days ahead of this catch, and now this one, that he wasn't going to %$@#! fish with me anymore, and then JP repeated the sentiment as he picked up his pack and rod on the bank. I laughed. "Come on, they were all *total luck!"* The ribbing continued. It was good to be on the water with great friends. But I told them the way I see it, JP brought me to this place, and Smitty gave me the fly. It was everyone's trout. Some days I'd rather be lucky than good. But I'd rather be lucky around good friends.

Angler's Circle of Life

A child sits on the end of a dock, feet dangling just above the water, a short superhero themed fishing rod with a hook, a worm, and some split shot to keep it down there. The child watches the little bluegills, the pumpkin seeds, the perch, as they hover around the worm, curiously staring it down, now and then a mouth puckering to bump the juicy thing. The child bounces the worm up and down, trying to force a take. The bait's raised slowly to see how far the fish will follow it up. Will they come right to the surface, will they stay down deeper. Will they think it's getting away and finally take it? On this day for whatever reason the fish just won't take the worm, and the child feels disappointment, a hint of things to come in life.

On the next day, attempting once again to become the master of nature several fish flail at the end of the child's line, and happiness and laughter carry across the water, the innocence of childhood not yet affected by the struggles of life. It's the child, the water, and the fish. The worms found under the boards behind the old shed and in the garden, an old metal tackle box filled with rusty old hooks and lures not yet understood but there waiting to be used. There is nothing else.

The child is growing older, learning new techniques at fooling fish, new knots to better secure a hook, and a better fishing rod has replaced the short kiddie pole of yesterday. The contents of the tackle box have been organized, new lures replaced the old, needle nose pliers reside in the bottom. Simply shaking a fish loose or stepping on the fish and yanking the hook out is no longer acceptable. The young person standing on the edge of the pond has seen the blood, has seen the fish floating on its side after being let go, and has learned to respect the fish a little more by using the pliers to carefully remove a hook, so that the fish can be caught another day. There's also a stringer, and if enough decent fish are caught, but not more than needed, and not out of season, his Grandfather will show him how to properly fillet the fish and his Grandmother will cook them for dinner.

He has mixed feelings on this. The catching is the fun, the catching is the challenge. The killing and eating is something else. It's a challenge unlike the rest of his life. It's not the challenge of learning to divide fractions in math, or the challenge of understanding how elements in the periodic table react together, and it's definitely not the challenge of interacting with other kids he can't seem to relate to. Catching a fish. This is the only challenge that leaves him to himself in his mind, the other challenges as important as they may be when he's not on the water, they're all unnecessary here, and a burden the mind needs not carry. The fish, the water, the immediate surroundings, these are all that matters. The killing of the fish weighs on his mind. The young person is slowly, through nature, learning to be a man.

A middle aged man finds himself at work yet again for the eighth day in a row, questioning. Everything he wants, a nice house, a good truck, maybe a little camp tucked away from everything on a lake somewhere, to get these things he has to work so many hours. So many hours spent making money to afford things that he has no time to enjoy because he's working all the time to afford them.
Each shift eight to twelve hours lost from his life, hours he never gets back. Day after day. This is being an adult? A man? This is a trap. Free men don't fall in traps. Slaves do.

On his day off, finally he hitches the boat up to the truck. He finds himself on a lake, the boat gently rocks on the water as he makes a cast to the end of a dock. He's hoping for a Bass to rush out and crush his streamer when the line goes tight. The tip of the rod dances as he strips in line, a life fighting him on the other end. He holds the large sunfish in his hands. Blues and greens and purples and oranges, the boat has drifted in to bump the end of the dock.

The fisherman looks down into the water and sees the small group of sunfish and perch hiding just in the shadow of the wooden structure and he smiles as he lets his catch return to the group. He hasn't thought about work, bills, or what needs to be done at home. In his mind he's sitting on the end of that dock, his feet dangling just above the water, a coffee can of worms beside him and some dirt spilled on the old wood next to it. He's a man who's found his way back to being a child.

The Lion King had the circle of life wrong. It's not about animals being born, dying, returning to the earth and then sustaining the next born. No. The circle of life, it's in fishing.

Gone Fishing

One day you're fishing five to six days a week, and the next thing you realize is you haven't made a cast in two weeks. You tell yourself its life, this is the way it is. But then you keep running that old and cliché saying across your thoughts, tearing them up like a monster truck over a field of tulips, *"Life is what you make it."* You can't get it out of your head anymore, you can't help but realize that life is short. *Too* short in fact to spend it chained to a job that gives you nothing but a paycheck, and takes everything else away.

And then one day sitting on the portaging bar of the canoe after releasing a good smallmouth, a 7wt fly rod at your side with a big meaty streamer trailing in the current next to the boat, you realize that this is your first fish in two weeks because of a job that takes all your personal time and flushes it down the toilet by either closing you up in a nasty factory or keeping you so tired from messed up shift work that you seem to do nothing but sleep. Not even good sleep, just a couple hours here and there, and about every week and a half you crash and sleep all day long.

The second thing you realize is that you're fishing, floating down a gorgeous stretch of river in complete silence, catching great fish, and thinking about how much you hate your job. You shouldn't be thinking about anything, now work is even taking that away from you.

At home you've got two lap tops opened up at the desk, and notebooks piled four high with still more pocket note pads, the cliché napkin with a story idea is buried somewhere in the mess, scraps of paper with notes scribbled, and a thesaurus opened to the page containing the word "meandering", trying to describe a stream for a story that should've been done three days ago. You've sent out stories to some magazines, *supposedly* one has been accepted but no checks have arrived yet and it's been bumped to *the next issue* once already. You won't be surprised when it happens the second time, you've got that nagging feeling it'll get bumped again.

You can't help but think that you could push harder and make things happen if you only had more time. But that's a poor excuse. It's always more something. More time, more money, a few more casts. But then you see people with even less time than you making it happen and you realize maybe you just need to buckle down and push harder. You wake up an hour later, the computer screen gone to sleep just like you, and it's time to go do something else. On your way out the door you tell yourself that the other day in the canoe you decided you should just quit your job. There's always another job somewhere else. You were looking for another job when you found this one after all. But the fish don't wait for you. They move around, they get caught by other fisherman, the seasons end. Life is too short. So what are you waiting for? Well, another job dummy.

Then it happens. You finish another chapter for a book about an Adirondack trout stream. You push out another story that you're really happy with, better late than never, and you send another one out hoping that someone at the magazine actually opens it and *reads* it. You fish two days in a row and feel good about getting skunked the first day and great about catching a single smallmouth on the second. It was a nice fish after all.

You have a positive outlook on life for a change. Maybe it's the support that your wife has been giving you with this whole writing thing, maybe it's listening to an eleven year old every morning on the ride to drop him off at baseball camp, rambling on about how great of a time he's having there, and maybe, just maybe, it's the fact that your buddy just found you a Monday through Friday day shift job and you know *this* Friday will be different.

At 11:30 Friday night you drop your last time sheet in the slot of the maintenance office. You load all your tools into the back of the Jeep. You throw away a pair of steel toe boots caked with grease, oil, and chemicals that most likely have been *proven to cause cancer in the state of California*, and you leave your hard hat in the top of an empty locker.

You're not retiring, you're just moving on to another job where you'll have time to live. In the morning when your last time sheet is removed from the box, there'll be no description of your hours and what you did on your last night. The message to the management will be loud and clear. Two words grace the time sheet. *Gone Fishing.*

The Dog Days of Summer

The dog days of summer are here. It's so dry, the creek has receded it's width to that of a small stream in several places, dry and white round stones exposed to the sun where there should be liquid flowing and hydrating the earth. Insects seem to float on a warm breeze more like the burning embers of a fire, riding the warm breeze wherever it may take them, rather than fluttering and buzzing about working to get somewhere. I can hear them sizzle as they pass in the baking UV rays cooking us all.

The water is cooler than the air no doubt, but as water temps of the creek go, it's very warm where it hardly moves, and only somewhat cooler where it gathers in deeper pools where I can see the fish lazily resting on the bottom seeking cool comfort and shelter from the warmth created by the sun light. As I lift my sun glasses to wipe sweat from my brows, I figure it's so hot, even the fish are sweating.

Nothing moves except the tiny bait fish, evidence enough for me that the larger fish, the bass I hoped to find are just not feeling it. The tiny minnows are left to feel safe and free in the wide open. Just as I lose my appetite for anything other than an ice cold beer on a scorching day in the sun, so have the smallmouths gathered in the deepest pools left on this stretch of the creek.

I think of the cold Utica Club cans in my fridge in the house. Besides a smallmouth that was maybe six inches and a fall fish about four, I've caught nothing today except for the sweat rolling into my eyes. On any other day I would've most likely, trying to reach a better casting position or merely convincing myself that I could make it to the far bank, fallen in by now. I do it quite frequently. Had I been born a Native American, the name given to me surely would have been "Falls in River."

I wore my waders today, not the brightest choice I've ever made, adding to the overheating issues, not wanting to bust through the dense undergrowth on my way to the water in shorts simply for a fear of the horrible ticks this season. I realize that even if I were to throw myself down into the creek at this point on purpose there isn't enough

127

of the warm water to make it above my waders and make any bit of a difference. What water that did get into them would most likely do nothing more than end up cooking me like bugs bunny in the kettle full of carrots and celery in the cartoons of my childhood, my waders serving as the pot holding the boiling water and the rabbit. I look to a small bird perched on a tree limb panting like a feathered dog in the heat... "What's up Doc?"

I make the decision to return home, and decide I should just strip down to my skivvies and collapse on the cool slate floor just inside my door way among the piles of work boots, my wife's shoes, and the kids baseball cleats and sneakers. Then I notice a couple miniscule splashes as I see tiny silver bodies break the surface in what looks to me a panic run. Without thinking, the glass fly rod sways and the sinking line and tiny gray streamer shoot out and land within inches of the activity still going on. Before I even have time to think I feel the slightest tug and then nothing. As I strip line twice more the tiny tug hits again and as I lift my leader from the water the corners of my dry and dehydrated lips curl up into a smile. I grasp the minnow that's only half again as long as the streamer that it finds itself attached to by its lip and as I drop it back into the water I again return to what the cool slate floor will feel like on my baking skin and the cold beer in the fridge.

It may rain in a couple days, then again, it may continue like this for another week. To stay home because I know I'm not going to catch anything is to accept defeat. I'll accept a skunk before I accept defeat in the confines of walls. These bass will eventually find something I toss irresistible, it's only a matter of time. And these hot summer days. They can only last so long before the bite is back on, no different than the iced over days of winter. The dog days of summer.

Cranberry Lake

I waded out about fifty feet from the shore line where our camp site met the water. I crossed a sandy bottom littered with scattered cobble stones, water logged branches and pine needles, and the occasional submerged chunk of drift wood in about waist deep water to get to the large boulder that hid just below the water's surface. I stood on the rock's flat top which put the water about half way up to my knees and looked up to the sun dropping toward the horizon on the opposite side of Cranberry Lake, hidden behind the clouds. This would be my last evening here, my last chance at a smallmouth at dusk.

Early in the morning I'd gotten up as the sun had just begun to lighten up the sky and paddled out about twice as far as where I now stood. I'd stripped out line and let it coil up at my feet as I stood in the canoe and doubted my abilities to bring a fish to hand in such conditions. The water was warm, I'd compared it to bath water upon our arrival the day before and had talked to a couple fisherman close by who'd caught nothing with worms. Surely if they caught nothing with worms, my 7wt and a foam popper would go unchecked by the bass trying to escape the summer heat in the depths.

But fish are merely my excuse, so with not much more thought, a foam frog popper tied a couple days before sailed back and forth over my shoulder before landing with a plop...And then disappearing in the hole in the water opened up under it by the mouth of the fish. A fish on my first cast without so much as even one strip of the line. How could I be so lucky? I laughed as I brought the fish to the boat. Some days it's better to be lucky than good. I missed one more strike then caught nothing for the next hour and a half before paddling back to camp.

JP always tells me that it's bad luck to catch a fish on your first cast, but It happens to me now and then like anyone else and to reason out the superstition in my head, I'd rather catch one on my first fish and then have the hope of another the rest of the day keep me going rather than to cast with nothing but doubt and desperation all day long only to catch one on the very last. Hope makes for a decent day. Desperation and doubt make for a less than completely enjoyable day. Still, I guess that would be better than work.

129

Now I stood perched atop the boulder, my back to the shore, the clouds gaining a slight tint of pink. Line fell in loose coils and floated on the water around my feet, once more the foam popper dangled at the end of the leader as I made a decision to start casting to my three o'clock position and working my way counter clockwise with successive casts covering the water as far out as I could. My first cast found nothing but water, as did my second. In fact my first complete rotation from three o'clock to nine showed no evidence that anything lurked beneath the surface at all. I didn't care. The fish are just the excuse.

The clouds gained color as I started back to my right again. I noticed Holly standing on the shore behind me and looked back. She smiled and I looked back to the water. As the loops passed overhead I wondered if she'd ever really watched me before and couldn't think of a time.

Lost in thought, between the strips and the popper throwing water I saw it disappear in a small splash and lifted the rod. There was resistance and then the green foam head launched from the water like a child flicking a rubber band at a classmate. "Ahhhh! Did you see it?" Holly chuckled no. It happened twice more before my wife asked me if I'd checked the point of my hook or if I was a half rate fisherman. My own *wife* busting *my* chops about missing hook sets. I *liked* it. The sun had illuminated the clouds to a strong pink by now and I was finding myself watching the bright ball of burning gases paint the sky deep hues as much as my fly line rolling across the open air.

At some point I realized that the large car sized boulders back along the shore behind me to my right had become somewhat of a set of rustic bleachers for the two couples and three or four teenagers who had the campsite next to us. They'd undoubtedly come out to view what was unfolding as one of the most stunning sun sets of the summer and I now realized that I too had become part of the show.

I could just hear key words of their conversation, which I'd picked up on in the background of them making references to a movie one of them remembered about a family who fly fished in Montana or someplace, and Brad Pitt. Then they moved onto what little they knew about the Adirondacks, who they knew that knew much more about them, and how it was the best $80 they'd ever spent for a place to stay on a vacation.

They seemed to think that the sunset and this guy out there casting graceful loops in a silhouette against the more and more gorgeous by the moment sunset was something special that demanded they keep their voices down to a gentle conversation...while my kids ran and yelled through the trees around our site like Indians raiding a wagon train camp in an old black and white western. I got a kick out of it but was lost in the spectacular sunset once again seconds later as the sun made a quick appearance between the clouds and the horizon before dropping below the trees and turning the clouds to a billowy canvas of purple and garnet.

I'd been casting nonstop and not taking one second of such a beautiful scene for granted for the better part of half an hour when finally the popper landed, I stripped twice, and as it sat motionless on the water it was smashed from below. I set the hook. The rod arched in the last minutes of the remaining light, I looked back to Holly still standing on the shore waiting for this moment and asked her if she was happy now that her husband had found a fish. At that same moment the audience on the boulders erupted like fans at a baseball game witnessing a good hit to the outfield and I couldn't help but smile.

Fly fishing is for me. I do it for myself, for my sanity, with many times a lack there of if you asked some of my family and friends. But this time it turned out I'd been a part of something bigger, I couldn't be so selfish this time. I waded in to shore with the smallmouth and let the kids feel its smooth scales and Holly took a picture while she smiled and the neighbors continued their comments and happiness filled their voices.

I know that all sounds very whimsical and a little mushy, but it's actually how it felt at the time, and I'm a writer and a fly fisherman, so you know I never exaggerate. I released the fish and made my way back out to my perch once more and continued fishing with no more luck until stars filled the sky and I had to feel my way back to the shore rather than look for my next steps.

There's a lot of things I'll never forget about my times with a fly rod in my hands. The first time I ever tried to cast. My first rod given to me by my father. The first fish. The first trout. My first custom rod. And that evening on Cranberry Lake in the Adirondacks when I was unknowingly sharing what I got out of it every time I went to the water with my wife and a group of perfect strangers because of one extraordinary sunset and an eleven inch bass.

I cast the fly rod for me. I'm selfish. But that evening everyone there felt what I felt. There's no way they didn't. It was a good thing. Something engrained in all our memories now. I'm sure.

The Lucky Fishing Shirt

I'm not a superstitious person. I don't care if a black cat crosses my path. As a matter of fact, I'll keep moving to the left so it has to keep crossing my path just to prove the point. I don't believe in the broken mirror thing. If you knew how many mirrors I shot in the old trash pile on the old farm behind my house as a kid, and then shot the broken pieces into smaller broken pieces, you'd see I'm serious about this whole anti superstition thing. Ladders? Yea, I'll walk under a row of twenty of them, just line 'em up. And I never knock on wood.

I've got this red t-shirt. Red, not a color that makes stalking fish in the clear small creek outback easy, but if I wear it out there, I still manage to catch fish. It's a Godzilla t-shirt. *"Godzilla. King of the Monsters."* He's got a menacing grin as he's tearing down a skyscraper and I had to have it when I found it at the store. It was the only one on the shelf, and it happened to be my size in a sea of other shirts all three sizes too big, so I thought it was just a mere coincidence, something finally going my way. My wife just laughed at me, but the kids thought it was cool. I loved it.

On our vacation a few weeks ago I was wearing the shirt while I was the only one off the campsite shore catching fish. I started to wonder. The clear creek out back at home in a bright red shirt, I catch fish. No one else here on the lake catching fish but me? The shirt? Maybe there's something to the whole superstition thing after all. But two instances wasn't enough to convince me.

In about 1989 I was a long haired head banger kid in ripped acid washed jeans on a secret family farm lake when I caught the biggest largemouth I'd ever caught, and that bass would hold the title for about twenty-six years. Just yesterday my father and I made the little over an hour drive south to the farm. For me it was now or never, do or die time. I hadn't made it there once this year yet, and this is the place that you just don't *not fish.* You get there at least once a year, and you fish. There's no arguing. You go.

I almost wore a long sleeved sun shirt, but at the last minute the Godzilla shirt was like a red beacon in a row of black and white fishing themed attire hanging in the closet. I threw it on, tossed the other shirt on the floor, and backed out of the driveway, the Toyota wearing the canoe like one of those goofy paper hats the cooks wore in 1950's diners.

Normally over the past couple years we'd show up early in the morning and leave midafternoon while the fishing was slow. This time we got there about noon, and managed a couple bass in the first ten minutes, just before the afternoon sun sent the fish to the locker room for half time. We'd missed the first half of the game, but I remarked to my father that I'd rather show up at half time with the chance to end the game with a good second half instead of playing the first half strong only to leave the game early not knowing how the second half ended. I refused to give up, keeping the fly line looping through the air most of the day, just staying in a rhythm if nothing else and enjoying a beautiful day on the sacred waters of my youth.

Then it happened. The sun started on its path towards the trees, and a sliver of shade began to appear and grow along the far side of the small lake. I looked at my father, pointed it out, and we paddled for different patches of shore line where the shade started to advance out across the water.

I'd been casting the glass 5wt with a small streamer and a sink tip, but looking at the shade and the water beginning to turn to glass, I set it to the side and picked up the 7wt with the frog popper and began hammering the weed bed that ran the entire shore all the way around the lake. It didn't take long before it happened.

The popper slapped down like it had the ten or so times leading up to this cast. I let it set motionless for a few seconds, and then three quick short strips threw water and advertised its presence. It sat motionless again. Just as I tensed up the muscles in my forearm for three more strips, the water opened up into a hole under the popper like the flushing of a toilet bowl and it disappeared. Cliché but true all the same.

In this lake you have to be fast in the shallows because the fish will dive straight down and bury themselves in the thick weed beds every time, and then it's a finesse game of working them back up and out, only for them to repeat the tactic over and over. I thought I had a normal sized twelve incher or so, stuck in the weeds as usual. Then something else happened.

Instead of just a tight line leading straight into the weeds motionless, the line began to vibrate like the cable of a crane lifting its maximum load, singing in pain, ready to stretch beyond its capabilities, and the fish actually started pulling line off my real as it muscled its way through the weed bed, like some huge grizzly bear charging through the brush unseen but making one hell of a racket on its path of destruction.

I didn't want to yell to my Father, who was now half way across the lake, that I had a big one, because there was still the chance in my head that it wasn't, but I couldn't say nothing either. At a time like this you have to get some kind of noise out of your mouth or you're bound to suffocate yourself holding your breath and pass out, so I hooted and hollered like a cow boy at the rodeo once and then pulled hard with a worried grin trying to remember if I had 6lb or 10lb tippet attached to the popper.

The 7wt was doubled over, like the St. Louis Arch, and the fish would make a run, half pull line and half try to pull the rod out of my hands as the canoe followed the path the fish brutishly swam as it bullied its way through the dark weeds on the bottom. In the end I had a largemouth that eclipsed my biggest ever, from this very same lake, within about 40yrds of the spot where the former had come from. I don't carry a measuring tape or a scale. I carry a camera and then memories for the rest of my times here in this life. We'll just say it was a *good fish*. I could stick my whole fist in its mouth.

And then there was the fact that I was wearing my Godzilla t-shirt. I guess I'll accept one superstition. This is my lucky fishing shirt. There's somethings you don't question. What rod should I use today? What fly? Streamer or dry fly? Wade or bank fish? Canoe or kayak? Call a fishing buddy or go alone? These are all acceptable questions. What shirt should I wear? *This* is no longer even a question. I'll either have to slow down my fishing, space out the days so that I have time to do laundry, or buy six more Godzilla t-shirts so that I have one for each day so that I can still fish all the time. This is my lucky fishing t-shirt...Somethings you just don't question.

Excuses

Sleeping bags were hung in the sun, draped over the canoe rack on my truck. My father's tent was set up not where he'd be sleeping in it by the fire but in front of my truck, also in the sun. Along with some clothes that were laid out on the hood or hanging from the canoe rack, everything, even my pack was emptied out and drying.

A hasty camp the night before while lost in the Adirondacks and the subsequent storm that rolled through had brought all of our gear to varying degrees starting at damp and ending at soaked. It was about noon, and we'd managed to find our way out of our predicament roughly an hour earlier. Instead of continuing on to where we wanted to go, we made the decision to drive out a couple miles the way we'd come in and to camp along a stretch of familiar river just off a dirt road, next to a bridge.

We should've been miles from anything manmade, instead we were feet from my Toyota and the bridge. Somethings just don't work out the way you want them to all the time I suppose, but two bumper stickers I once saw always hover around in my mind when I'm on the water and things aren't going exactly as I'd planned. *Any day above ground is a good one,* and *A bad day fishing is better than a good day at work.* While water evaporated from damp clothes in the sun, I strung up my 3wt. We weren't going to lose any more time fishing.

The storm the night before had the river running a little high, a little faster, and as I waded out into the water I searched with my feet for places to wedge my wader boots in between rocks to anchor myself before my first cast. I stripped line from the small reel and sent the white marabou streamer to a pocket about fifteen feet out from me. Landing it just above the boulder braking the water, it washed down around the near side and into the slack water on its downstream side and I mended the line with a quick lift of the rod to hover the false bait fish in place for a second longer before giving it life.

On the first small strip in the pocket the brookie appeared from below in haste and turned back to the bottom, my line going tight. I lifted, the rod tip bent, then went limp. I let the streamer drift and

137

swim downstream and swing across below me and as I stripped it back to me another strike in more turbulent current, this time the rod tip bent and a fish was brought to hand. No more than 6" or so, its colors were brilliant. Bright pink spots with a halo of light blue, orange and yellow dots against almost black par marks above a bright rusty orange belly. Its fins trimmed in pure white, and a camouflaged back, if there was a fashion show for fish, surely the brook trout would the cat walk like a super model.

All day while gear dried and bugs bit, the fish were willing, and my streamer became more ragged as the day passed by. My father on the other hand didn't have quite the same luck. Lately it seems that on still water, lakes and ponds, he'll out fish me on most any day, and on a trout stream, our roles reverse. But whichever one of us is having the slow day, you probably wouldn't know it by the looks on our faces. My father sat on a rock at one point, water flowing past him on all sides, his fishing rod idle. Just taking in the scenery all around and listening to the river, I could see where he and I are alike, at least on the water.

Some people find all the excuses why they can't go fishing. "I have to mow the lawn. I have to change the oil in the car. I have to get some work done on the house. I need new line for my rod. I'm out of flies. I'm too busy." I brought another fish to hand and studied the varying colors and shades as I had on the previous fish, no two looking the same, but all of them quite spectacular in their own way. And there was my father, not having caught anything over a few hours, yet resting atop a boulder with content on his face, observing everything around him. And that's where we're alike.

We don't make excuses about why we can't get out to fish, and when we're out we don't get upset about getting skunked. Instead of making excuses, the fish *are* our excuses. The excuses we use to get out and enjoy being out and away from the hustle of everyday life. The excuse of the *fish* is what gets us to these beautiful places, disconnects us from the stress of modern living, and connects us to what is important. Us.

The Last Days of Trout Season

It's the last week of trout season in NY, and I find myself hopping rocks on the Black River below North Lake in the Adirondacks. I've come here in search of small and wild brook trout while most everyone else I asked to come along gave the excuse of "Why would I want to go looking for those *little fish* while the *Salmon* are starting to run up in Pulaski?" Truth be told, none of them are on the Salmon River that weekend. The excuse they use for not wanting to come along on a fishing weekend is big fish that they've got no intention of actually going after. They sit at home and watch reality TV. They'll do yard work. They'll get the snow blower ready for winter. On Monday morning at work when someone asks them what they did over the weekend their answer will be *not much*. Their loss, my gain. I feel bad for them, but because I'm alone it's quiet and I can fish as long as I want, and go upstream as far as I please without worrying if someone else is tired or hungry or cold. That's a win in my book.

I've brought to hand half a dozen small brookies, most around the seven inch mark. A lot of people would call them natives. Are they? I couldn't tell you. Most likely they're lineage has something to do with a hatchery at some point, simply because the lake this water flows from was once dead like a lot of lakes in the Adirondacks from acid rain. They're most likely *not* native trout, but they're wild. This I can tell you from catching some down around three inches. They don't stock them that small which tells me, stocked at one time or not, these fish are reproducing in the wild, which makes them wild fish in my book. Their fall colors are as bright as the falling leaves all around me, their black eyes like peering into black holes reaching all the way back to prehistoric times. The brook trout, unlike the invasive brown that was brought here from overseas, was here long before us, and with any luck will still be in the Adirondacks long after we've gone.

As I stand on a boulder the size of a Volkswagen Bug with water flowing three-hundred and sixty degrees around me, I inspect the brown Woolly Bugger tied to my tippet. It looks ragged after a day of bouncing down the stream bottom, after being dragged across uncountable submerged boulders and logs, and gnashed at by teeth. I

139

open my fly box and my eyes scan across my staple of flies I never leave home without on a trip like this. Small black and brown nymphs, two rows of them. Tied in various designs, I copy none of them straight out of a tying book. I just make "buggy things". They work now and then.

One row of dries is it, a few Mayflies and March Browns and a couple Black Ants. I'm not a good dry fly fisherman anyhow so what good would having anymore do me is the way I see it. On a trip like this I rely mostly on the Wollybuggers. Blacks, browns, and olives, they look like a meal to me, and the fish often agree. I close the box up, why change it now. It's still working.

The short 3wt rod is perfect out here and every cast just seems *right*. The rod dances as another brookie darts out from behind a small boulder in a pocket and realizes it's been had a second too late. Such a gorgeous small wild fish in such a wonderful place. If content could be spelled by pictures instead of letters, this would be it.

Tonight I'll cook walleye over the fire caught the weekend before specifically for this outing, and I'll sleep in a tiny pup tent not a dozen feet from the river's edge. Tomorrow morning my Father will join me on this small piece of chilly October paradise. But for now, as I hop from rock to rock on my way back downstream to my camp site, I'll try a few more casts to the pockets I missed on my way up. Why indeed would I want to be here when the Salmon are running? I pray to God that no one ever figures the answer out.

A Worthy Fish?

On a social media fly fishing page this past week I came across someone who'd posted up a picture of a decent sized carp. There were a couple "Nice carp" and "Great fighters" responses to the photo, but within the first four reactions to the golden scaled tank of a fish there was one guy who posted "Garbage fish. Throw it on the bank for the birds." Most everyone ignored him, a couple didn't, but it led me to the question of what qualifies a fish as worth catching?

Carp have long been considered a trash fish by many, it's only recently become somewhat of a game fish, and I believe a lot of that has to do with the progression of fly fishing and those who chase bigger fish with bigger rods. But why does a trout get the love and a carp gets the evil eye? Let's compare them.

Trout are very picky. Whatever they key in on, that's about all you're going to catch them on, most of the time anyhow. Carp can be the same way, perhaps even more mysterious to figure out. Trout can be caught on anything from a tiny nymph to a long streamer. Same with carp. As a matter of fact, the same flies that will catch trout will catch that huge golden tank that fights like a log with an attitude. And for the record, if you fight a carp for five minutes, it's still fighting to get out of your hands and take off, while the trout that fights for five minutes is ready to die. And the carp is found in the same waters, and then in waters much worse, waters a trout could never live in. Yet the trout gets all the fame and the carp gets asked to use the back entrance.

And on a final trout vs carp note, just to piss some people off, if you're talking about brown trout here in the U.S. don't start spouting how the carp is invasive... Because so are the browns. They were brought over from Europe and pushed a lot of native fish out of their waters. But hey, they're trout, not carp, so for whatever reason it's cool right?

How about the fall fish vs. the smallmouth bass? I honestly believe, as much as I love chucking streamers for smallies, and as many times that I've stated my beliefs that the smallmouth is the hardest fighter pound for pound, that the fall fish... a large minnow, may *actually* be the hardest fighter pound for pound. But it gets no love at all. At least

141

there *are* tournaments and records for carp now. The only time I hear talk of fall fish are when I hear fishermen complaining that they caught no trout or smallmouth, only bottom feeders, or suckers or creek chubs as they're most commonly misidentified. Why is that? They share the same water, they eat all the same foods, they're caught on all the same flies and lures, and they fight like a ticked off bull at the rodeo with a rope tied tight around his unmentionables! Yet they get no love!

And while we're on the subject of "*bottom feeders*", why is it that carp, fall fish, whitefish, sheepshead, why are they all trash fish because they're considered bottom feeders, but the catfish is cool? All these fish eat the same things, they can all be found in many of the same waters, yet only some are worthy of chasing while others aren't?

I guess it's just a human thing. We do it to ourselves, separating races and stereotyping, so why shouldn't we do it to fish too? To me, the same guy that would throw a fish on land because it was a "garbage" fish is probably the same guy that leaves his trash behind at the water's edge and poaches fish out of season and ignores limits. No respect for his surroundings.

I go fishing to escape the human world. And I guess treating every fish as an equally good opportunity to enjoy nature is part of leaving humans behind for short periods of time on the water. Tomorrow I'm going after pike, but I won't be disappointed to find its smaller cousin the pickerel on my streamers. Don't even get me started on the whole pickerel thing...

Fishing Trucks

The truck floats down the road five miles an hour above the speed limit. *Floats* is the word I choose to describe the ride only because it feels more like a boat on the water than a vehicle on smooth blacktop. The shocks are gone. Shot. They may as well not even be bolted to the frame at this point they're so worthless. I sweep through a corner, the road dips, and the boat feels like it might roll too far and capsize on the next wave. Two hands on the wheel. I'm fine with it. The check engine light's lit up, telling me something stupid is wrong, like some emissions sensor, the catalytic converter, the exhaust leak I know is there in the rusty old pipe under the passenger floor boards, or the fuel filler neck for the gas tank has come loose again. The truck runs fine. I drive on.

Inside the cab Iron Maiden wails through old cracking speakers, drowning out the creaks and metallic sounds of loose stuff underneath, the vibrations in the dash that a swift smack of a fist from above will no longer quiet. The only thing the smack of my hand fixes now is the electric window switches when the driver's door window decides it won't move anymore and when the left side of the dash gauges go dark at night. Either one of these problems can still be remedied with a clenched fist and a well-placed blow of flesh on plastic. I'm an excellent mechanic.

This truck has logged some serious miles getting me to fish, and it's always stocked and ready for the next adventure. Yea, it may be my daily ride to work, but this is my fishing truck.

It's been a faithful friend for ten years now, always getting me to the fish, or at least to the trail head, never leaving me standing by it on the side of the road cussing it out like so many other 4x4s in my past. But there comes a time where you begin to look at old friends and wonder *how did we get to this point*?

That point came to me a few months ago when I pulled into my wife's parking lot to bring her dinner one afternoon. She goes in midafternoon to work and leaves later than others which means she ends up parking way out in the boonies. It was a simple question she asked after she walked up to the truck and I lowered the driver's side window, passing her the white Styrofoam container and giving her a kiss. "Can you give me a ride out to the far corner of the parking lot so I can move my car closer?" My answer brought on that point of which I'm discussing. "Sure" And then with a glance to the passenger seat mounded with waders, a net, a couple rod tubes and fly boxes, "But you'll have to sit in the back." Her grin was a mixture of *I know* and *we've spoken about the condition of your truck before*. I quickly followed it up with "I love you" accented by a Cheshire cat smile. Then she proceeded to push the contents filling the back seat over to make room. More fly rod tubes. An extra pair of boots. A small stack of fly fishing magazines tipping and spreading out like a dropped deck of playing cards. More fly boxes, tippet packages and a chest pack. It was an awkward sixty second ride.

The responsible adult somewhere inside me would tell you that my truck is first and foremost my means of getting to work, of earning a paycheck. Its other roll of picking the boys up at school could be viewed as equally important. But that would all be true if only you could find that responsible adult somewhere inside me. No, if you asked and I was being honest, the trucks job is to carry me on fishing excursions near and far and it should run well enough to also get me to work in-between said fishing excursions. Hey, at least I know deep inside that I've got *my* priorities straight. The proof would be if the truck was to puke all of its contents into my driveway if I were ever to clean it out.

Under the seats you'd find needle nose pliers long MIA, replaced time and time again on the way out of town to chase scales. A hatchet. Maps with water stains, ink blurred by dampness and permanent wrinkles from rainy days of fishing trips past. A plastic divided tackle box the size of which might fit in a pants cargo pocket peaks out from underneath the passenger seat. Filled with Meps spinners, it remains from my last days of the spinning rod. I haven't cast one in at least four years, yet the box remains. Removing it would somehow feel like amputating my little toe for no reason. It does me no good, yet it's a part of me and part of the truck. To lose it would seem a tragedy for some strange reason. To question these things too deeply is to peer into one's own sole. The tackle box stays.

Magazines originally were tucked into the pockets on the backs of the front seats with maps, a couple odd assorted wrenches and tools settled in the bottom clanking now and then as the truck slams pot holes and strays to rough road shoulders. But the literature now slides across the back seat, sometimes coming to rest on the floor. I swap them out now and then with the one in my tool box at work. Variety is the spice of life they say. The truck is the typical means of conveyance for many a diehard angler, but there's one thing that's drawn a couple odd looks once it was realized what exactly it was that was going on in the bed.

I mounted a large steel locking job site storage box in the bed, originally meant to be the world's biggest fly box ever. In an upper shelf could be found foam panels cut to fit, stocked up with flies for every condition and location. From huge streamers to tiny dries and everything in between. The Boy Scout moto of "Be Prepared" never goes unfulfilled. In the bottom of the box, securely locked away and always there and ready were fly rod tubes. A 3wt, a 5wt, and a 7wt always on board. A pair of waders appropriate for the season, an extra pair of boots and socks, a couple nets, a wading stick, a back pack stocked with camping and survival necessities, a cast iron skillet and some dry kindling and firewood. But once the cooler weather moved in the box transformed.

I had a friend bringing me buck tails all hunting season. This past year I decided to collect as many as possible and dye them for tying. Cleaning and drying them in the garage, the smell of which wasn't going to fly with the wife, didn't seem like an idea that was going to work out well in the short game. She'd get over it sooner or later, but in the short game, well, you know how it goes. *Happy wife, happy life*. So I needed a place to clean the tails and dry them. The gear was removed from the box, the tails were cleaned and treated on the tailgate in the driveway, and the shelf in the box became the drying rack. A mobile drying rack. It raised a couple questioning looks, and a couple guys thought it was just cool as hell. My redneck points sky rocketed that day. I haven't decided if that's good or bad.

But all good things must come to an end. I found myself transferring the license plates off the old Toyota and onto an even older Jeep this past week. The difference is the Jeep was taken care of while the Toyota, well, let's just say I got my money out of it. It still runs like a sewing machine, if sewing machines had rotten bumpers, rusty shocks, and as my wife puts it, smelled like fish inside.

I swear I'm going to keep the Jeep clean. I won't fill up the interior with piles of smelly fishing gear. I won't keep three-hundred pounds of stuff I really don't and won't ever need inside, and I'll keep an air freshener hanging from the mirror. One of those little pine tree deals. All I need on board is my cassette tapes and sunglasses. The rest can stay in the house until needed.

But spring is on its way, and the creek could clean up to fishable levels any day now, so I should probably stick the 5wt and a small box of nymphs and streamers in the back for that stop on the drive home in the mornings. And I should have a net in there too. And I should probably put needle nose pliers in the glove box for the times I forget them, just to be safe. Extra nippers too. And really, the space behind the back seat in a Cherokee is so big, there's plenty of room for a plastic tote to keep my waders and boots in. Yea, that's all I need. I shouldn't need anything more except... Listen, I promise you'll never see animal parts hanging and drying inside the back windows. Promise.

Fly Fishing is Emotion

It begins in the shop of the rod maker. The time spent designing. The ideas thrown around about materials and components. They're all personal choices to both the rod maker and the customer for whom this 9' 5wt is intended. Blood, sweat, tears. Anguish over the smallest details goes into the build, an expression of the artist, an extension of the angler. Perhaps a little scotch as the rod dries. The rod maker is an artist, and art is self-expression. It's their way of giving to those around them, of letting peers hopefully feel a little of what the artist feels.

It continues on the first time the owner first sets eyes on their new rod. They pour over the details, taking in all the hard work, the perfection of the wraps, the gloss of the finish. The feel of smooth cork in their hand. The engraving. This was done for *them,* not for the random person to find on a store rack with dozens of other identical rods.

But it's most likely found in no greater amounts than on the water, in the hands of the angler. The angler stands knee deep in a slow current which calms the soul and ignites the imagination both at once. The rod is held at their side, as if they were standing there taking in the view with an old friend. The angler strips line, estimating what he believes to be enough to reach his desired distance, where the fish of his dreams lays in wait. Even the fly tied to his tippet. The fly he agonized over the night before, selecting the perfect hackle, the correct size and color. Even the tiny fly is part of it.

The cast is quite possibly the part of it that everyone feels, even the non-fishermen. The grace in the movements. The sway and the arch of the rod as it's loaded by the line on the back cast. The loop. The flow of the line as it unrolls elegantly before the angler and is rocketed forward racing through the guides before its energy is finally spent, the fly falling quietly to the water's surface.

As the fish rises and sips in the delicate dry fly and turns for the bottom, the rod is lifted and dances in the angler's hand. It dances because it's happy. Fly Fishing, is emotion.

Old Enough to Know Better

I was walking across the dirt parking area, waders making that familiar zip zip sound of friction with each step, calling out the cadence of the skunked angler as I marched back to the Jeep. I'd been the only vehicle in the lot when I'd parked over an hour ago, but now there sat a small pick up next to my new-old ride, and the guy behind the steering wheel smiled and nodded as I walked up to the back door.

"That's a real nice rig you got there, I saw you in town a few days ago and had to pull in here when I saw it parked to check it out." I smiled and said Thanks, unlocking the door and tossing my net in the back and leaning the fly rod against the spare tire. "I have to ask, since it's lifted and has the winch and all, why you didn't go with a more aggressive mud tire?" I smiled and chuckled and did my best at a short but to the point answer. "Well, I just bought this thing a couple weeks ago, and these were on it. But honestly I don't think I would've put anything much more aggressive on it because, well, I had mud trucks when I was younger…And I broke them…A lot. I don't think I'll be doing much mudding with this one, I just wanted some ground clearance and a nice Jeep. They were fun when I was younger, but I'd like to think I'm old enough to know better now." He laughed and agreed, said he understood completely.

For the record, I'm that guy that could never have anything nice, and most of the time it was my own doing.

As I pulled onto the pavement my own words kept echoing in my head. *Old enough to know better*. Wow, did I really say that? I could only think of one place that I'd need the Jeep's ground clearance to get to a fishing spot. The family farm meant trekking across old pastures riddled with boulders and stumps hidden in waist high neglected hay fields. Pretty much any of my other fishing spots were at most a drive on a washboard seasonal dirt road that you were liable to pass a two wheel drive family sedan on, never once needing to drop the transfer case lever into 4 high let alone run out the winch cable.

Are there places I'll go to and eventually need the lift and the winch? Sure. Probably. Maybe. But I broke a lot of parts on my lifted trucks

148

when I was young... I'd like to avoid that now, this being my only vehicle. It's got to get me to work. Growing up *absolutely* takes the fun out of quite a few things you took for granted when you were younger.

Old enough to know better. What do I really, truly need to get me to the fish? I think back to some of the cars and trucks my younger brother Luke has had, and one pops to the front. I met him one day at Delta Lake, the plan was to head out in his canoe and chase largemouths and pickerel in the back sets. He was bringing the canoe.

Now he's had quite the eclectic fleet of vehicles over the years, from Bronco II's with tree trunks for bumpers and no doors to 1980's Firebirds with no doors. No, really, it was a Firebird and it had no driver's door...at all. I'm not really sure what it is he had against doors, but it was a reoccurring theme at least twice in his fleet, which unless you're talking Jeeps, is two more times than you've probably known anyone else to lose perfectly good doors. But on this outing he pulls to the shoulder of the road in a white sedan, an older Acura that looked like a mule that had been beaten and whipped within an inch of its life. A mule would have been able to defend itself at least, they bite and kick.

This poor, once luxury sedan couldn't do anything except defecate transmission fluid and rust on the shoulder of the road in fear, while it was abused to the tune of an old, and ironically much nicer, green canoe strapped to its once sleek and smooth roof line. The roof crumpled, and the sail panels connecting the roof to the quarters buckled under the stress of the ratchet straps hooked into the rotted wheel openings. I remember wondering whether I'd back way off in traffic behind it or if I'd try to speed up and get around it. It was impressive. In a sort of scary, backwoods, hillbilly kind of way.

A quick glance inside would've had most people back peddling. Leaning in to glance at the interior I saw something that could have been best described as what looked like a yard sale full of old fishing and hunting gear. One of those yard sales that never seems to end. You know, the one you pass every year on the way to the lake, half the tables covered in old tarps, a permanent yard sale sign pounded into the ground with weeds growing up all around it and the letters faded because the yard sale has been going on for five years now. You never stop.

I can still picture the cracked and weathered tan leather seats, the back seat and floor boards were a pile of sleeping bags, jackets, fishing rods, tackle boxes, an old wood stocked pellet gun, some turkey feathers laid on the back dash under the glass fading in the sun. An old minnow trap and short ice fishing rod hid in the pile behind the drivers' seat. I can guarantee you there was an ax in there somewhere if you had the guts to reach in and start digging around. Everything had a damp look to it, like it had all been rained on recently, just not today.

On the front floor board was a full squirrel tale with a huge hook at the end and a spinner blade at the front. "That's gonna get me a big ol' pike" he said as he noticed my gazing at the damp animal appendage on the passenger floor board. "I love the leather seats too" he said without missing a beat. "The water and mud wipes right off of them." Right off them and onto the floor he meant. There were boot prints in the mud on the driver's side. Not *muddy boot prints*, no. Boot prints in the mud. In the car. I was impressed. The car looked like it had been through Hell and back, and looked like it would've probably been in a better place if it had just stayed there.

But he was doing everything that I plan on doing with this Jeep with that old, mostly used up, two wheel drive, once luxury sedan meant for the pavement and nights on the town. Fishing, camping. Hauling canoes and scaring little old ladies. No lift kit. No big tires. No winch. No four wheel drive.

As I pulled off my waders at the front door I looked at the Jeep sitting there all tall and tough in the driveway. I admitted to the guy in the dirt lot that I'd probably never do any real serious wheeling with it to get to my fish. I thought about my brother and how he probably took that poor car to places it should have never been able to go. Did I *really* need this Jeep like I said I did, the ultimate fishing rig to get me there? A lift kit, big tires, a winch, the rod rack on the roof? Of course not. I'm old enough to know better. But apparently I'm still too young to care.

All Winters Must End

I shoveled a path to the grill through a foot and a half of heavy, wet snow. As I stood there grilling burgers and sipping on a porter in a long sleeved t-shirt I couldn't help but smile. I could finally hear the current of the creek, the ice melting away in several small patches enough for the water to call out to me, to let me know it would be ready soon.

As we finished our dinner, Holly says to me "You can go fishing for a little bit if you want, the boys will be leaving for religion class soon anyhow. I shrug my shoulders. "I don't know, maybe." I clean my plate at the sink and look out at the sun shining, the bright orange ball of fire hangs just above the trees and the frozen creek. The thermometer says it's 52. I slap myself in the face. "You idiot, this is what you've been waiting for all winter. You can't catch fish if you're not fishing."

Where the creek out back ends and flows into the Mohawk River I find myself standing in knee deep snow, breathing heavy from the walk in. Winter waders are cumbersome enough even before you have to push a hundred yards though knee deep snow. The creek is still frozen over, but the ice is thinning.

The Mohawk however is clear. Ice free. I can fish the creek for trout, it's one of the few waters in the state that's open year round for catch and release trout fishing. But of course it's iced over. The Mohawk on the other hand is wide open, the water a light tea stained color and running high from the melting snow. It holds trout, but merely feet away from the creek which feeds it, trout season is closed on this river.

I tie on a four inch white and red streamer with holographic eyes. There's four more days of walleye and northern pike season before it closes for a month. What have I got to lose? Daylight. That's about it. And a streamer. Perhaps the feeling in my toes as I stand in knee deep snow on the side of the river. It's been two months since I last cast the 6wt. It seems like two years. Until the first cast, then it feels like it was only yesterday.

The fly glides and twitches perfectly. I've never fished with the sinking line yet, but after a couple casts I decide I can deal with it. My thoughts

151

are shattered by the "whack" and violent splash in the river in front of me. Not the pike I had hoped would cause the commotion, but a beaver has decided I should leave. I reel in the line as the last of the sun filters through the trees and I sit in the snow. Neoprene wader boots and a fly rod, my legs stretched out, my butt settled into the cold white stuff. A river just past my toes pointed to the sky and a sun setting to my back. Just like a day at the beach...Minus the sand in my shorts. Life is good on the water.

The April Fools

It could be said that the opening of trout season in New York State sharing the same day as April Fools has got to be either one of the most ironic coincidences ever to mark a square on a calendar, or one of the greatest jokes to ever be told of which most people plainly miss the punch line. Hordes of anglers get up early, race to the river to claim their spot on the bank, and become one of a hundred lines in the water attempting to fool fish that for the most part, only days earlier, were living in what could best be described as a swimming pool. Born and raised in this rectangular concrete pond, these same fish are now either hunkered down in the deepest hole in the middle of the river wondering what the hell is going on or running a gauntlet of nearly invisible monofilament, spinners, power baits, and flies.

At a spot like this, there's generally three types of anglers present. Those who will "limit out" on fish that were just too dumb or merely unlucky enough to fall for a joke being played out literally all around them would be the first type. Opposing them would be the anglers who'll release every trout they catch, knowing in their mind that each fish set free helps to ensure the future of the fishery for both the fish and future anglers. Third are the anglers who won't catch a single fish but will offer up the wisdom that any day spent fishing whether catching or not is a day spent enjoying the outdoors and better than a day doing anything else.

The first group will think they're the smartest because, well, they're the ones with the full stringer. The second will think they're the smartest because they're the ones without a stringer, and the third think they're the smartest because they believe they've discovered the secret to life. No matter how you slice it, mind sets and opinions aside, they're all getting beaten at some point by an animal with a brain the size of a pea. April Fools.

But the fools aren't only stacked on river banks like cord wood on the edge of town. No, some of us feel that if we get up even earlier, drive a lot farther, and find a piece of water where we'll be the only ones there, that we must be the smarter ones. We might find wild fish, but we might not with just as much work. We still get beat by animals with pea brains, we just exerted a little more effort into it. And we also think we're the smarter ones. I can't really relate to those fisherman all gathered in one spot competing for the same ten inch stocked fish, but I can't hold it against them either.

What I *can* relate to is that they're fishing, and fishing means they aren't dealing with any of the other BS going on around us daily that we have no control over like politics, race riots in faraway cities, religion, or the idea of global climate change, let alone a *job*. Whether shoulder to shoulder or out of sight on a hidden stream or lake, anglers know they need to escape such things or else become just another lemming bound to eventually follow the rest of the group over a cliff. So we go fishing.

The past couple months of being cooped up inside and bombarded with election campaigns might shed a little more light on the situation. I just don't care anymore. Whatever it is they have to say, I don't care. The rich will always be rich, the poor always poor. Politicians will always speak in riddles or all out lies. No one will ever agree on anything. I don't care who sits in the oval office, these things will always remain constant. Always have, always will. The fact that just as we've all had enough of the useless banter from the puppets behind the podiums, that something like trout season comes along to sweep us all away tells me that someone else once also had enough and decided to do something about it. They decided to go fishing too. They'd had enough as well.

I find myself as I get older having a harder and harder time relating to the rest of the world and its problems. I've been accused of becoming anti-social, and I'm sure there's some truth to that. I don't care to argue about politics, foreign policy, racism, religion, or global warming. I'm not saying they aren't important discussions, I'm just saying they were here before me, they'll still be here when I'm gone, and it's the stuff that you have no control over that'll eat you up if you give it the chance.

I do however have control over the loop of my fly line, at least some of the time. I can't relate to the rest of the world as easily these days. I seem to be able to relate to the fish better. Like them, I just want to be

154

left alone. So as irony would have it, I go out on my own to find them. Just another fool shivering with frozen fingers in a freezing cold river, wondering if there are even any trout in it at all. On April first. Another April fool.

Where the Fish Are

A few e-mails during the week had set up our first outing of the 2016 trout season. On opening day I was driving north, the Jeeps windshield wipers slashing through a steady rain to a Dire Straits song when the gas station on the way in to the town of Old Forge came into view. It wasn't the one I was meeting JP and a friend of his that I hadn't met yet at, but I'd just come off the midnight shift less than an hour ago so I needed some gas station coffee and breakfast pizza.

On the way back out the doors the guy in front of me held the door open and we both kind of shook our heads and laughed as the rain started to fall a little harder. He looked back at me, "I'm meeting a couple friends up here to go fishing, great day for that." I chuckled. "Yea, me too. Great first day of the season, I'm wondering if the guys I'm supposed to meet will even show up or if I drove up here for nothing." He echoed something along the same lines in agreement, then as we both climbed in our vehicles I shouted over the rain hammering the roofs "Just remember when you're standing in the woods all by yourself because you were the only one dumb enough to not stay home, I'll be standing out there somewhere too thinking the same thing. Good luck!" I drove on to the next gas station another half hour north, chewing on an hour old slice of pizza, sipping a bitter coffee because I'd forgotten the sugar.

As I pulled into the EZ Mart in Inlet, I laughed and shook my head as the Silverado pick-up from the last gas station, driven by the guy who'd shared his concerns over being the only one crazy enough to show up, pulled in next to me. We looked at each other though blurry glass covered in cascading rain water and smiled. So we were only missing JP now. John and I stood under the overhang outside the door and introduced ourselves and talked for a few minutes before JP pulled up. We shared our story about the first unofficial meeting at the other gas station, then we all pulled on waders in the comfort of a dry store and pointed our front bumpers north once more to finish the drive.

Parked on the side of a dirt road we strung up rods, the rain had tapered off to a light drizzle. It was an unusual spring in the north country. Normally on April 1st if you wanted to hike into one of these small streams for brookies you'd need snow shoes. Except for the tiny patch of white about the size of a door matt in front of my Jeep there was nothing. We weren't complaining, at least about snow. As we began our walk in on a small game trail that seemed to go the right direction the rain picked up again. Oh well. When you've driven an hour and a half and your waders are on and your rod is strung up and your parked miles down a dirt road you're pretty much committed, not that I'd ever turn around *anyhow*.

If it wasn't for the narrow game trail, even though nothing green had started to grow and take over yet, walking in would've been nothing short of a near impossible bushwhack. Once we got to the water we traveled upstream a ways to find the big pools that JP wanted to scout out. It was pretty cold, but if I kept moving I didn't notice all that much. And the trees and ground cover grabbing my rod tip or snagging my tippet every ten feet or less kept my mind off the cold. That and as usual, the scenery.

I'm distracted each time I venture into a remote piece of the Adirondacks like this by the fact that I suddenly feel small in the world, that even though I may be with someone else, I feel alone, and alone never felt as good as each time I feel it in a place like this. The brook trout brought me here, they don't care about the rain, they're already wet. Therefore somehow because of them, or through them, I don't care about the rain either.

Golden Dorado in Argentina. Trout in New Zealand. Permit in Belize. Salmon in Alaska. Bone fish in the Bahamas. Pike in Saskatchewan. Tarpon in the Keys. Taimen in Mongolia. Tiger fish in South Africa. I don't know where I'm going with this list, other than I've been pretty adamant about the fact that it's not always the fish, but the places that they take you. I've never seen any of these fish in any of these places.

The Adirondack brook trout, a trophy at eleven inches in small streams, is *my* "getaway" fish. At the end of last year I caught my biggest trout on the fly, a really nice brown that was a healthy and heavy eighteen inches. But it felt more like a twenty incher, so we'll just say it was twenty-two. I always used to joke that I hoped I never caught a big trout because I was afraid from that point on I'd compare the little

157

brookies to it and they'd seem less important.

Last week I caught my first trout of the year, a wild brookie about nine inches give or take. It was a pretty fish, from a remote stream in the Adirondacks. The place is full of history and fish. And skinny water. *Cold* skinny water. I was standing in water up to my waist in the pouring rain, JP was scouting ahead looking for a pool on the map, and John was making his way upstream and across, braving the freezing tea colored water like me.

At some point I realized that having only worn my light waders and no thermals or anything, I was a moron. And I was *very* cold. My legs were stinging. But the sting gave that burning sensation, and as we all know, burning is warmth. So I told myself that in all reality, I was warm. I made the best of it, caught a fish, and got the hell out of the water. I never once thought of the last trout I landed before this one, my biggest ever, so I'd say my theory about ruining smaller fish is a bust. My theory that it's the places as much as the fish *must* be true.

I'd still like the chance to toss big meaty streamers at tiger fish in South Africa. Or golden dorado in Argentina. And now I think I can say that I'm sure they could never take the place of my little brookies. They'd just be other places and other fish. But you've got to be satisfied with what you have and what you can do or you'll never be happy. Somebody told me that once, they're right, but I still hate them for saying it.

The Older I get the Better I Was

In my mind it seems to have been a lot simpler when I was a kid. Fishing that is. It's funny how your outlook on things changes as you get older, what you saw then, and what you see looking back now. A typical fishing excursion back then, let's say in about the eighth grade, would've been a spinning rod and a small plastic tackle box. One of those boxes with plastic dividers, stocked with a mix of soft plastic worms, jigs, spinner baits, and the classic and sure bet bass slayer, the Hula Popper. I never left home without a Hula Popper.

If you don't know what a Hula Popper is there can only be two excuses. One would be that you've never done anything but fly fish, that you never picked up a spinning rod, and that I could accept. The other excuse would be that you've never fished, that you've had your head somewhere it doesn't belong for your entire life, and that most likely you and I would never have anything in common to talk about. I'd also question why you'd be reading this if you hadn't the faintest idea as to what one was. Let's just say it's a hard plastic thing that may or may not resemble a frog wearing a grass skirt, with treble hooks. Moving on.

I'd head out the door with the spinning rod, the small tackle box, a pair of needle nose pliers swiped from a mess of rusty tools left on the garage floor, work boots, jeans, a baseball cap, a pocket knife, and a big ass survival knife on my side. The pliers were obviously for removing hooks from fish and fingers, and the work boots and jeans were because I wasn't going to get all bit up by ticks and mosquitos. And as a long haired 80's head banger kid I wasn't going to be caught dead in shorts.

The pocket knife was to cut fishing line tangles and whatever other small blade work might present itself, and the big ass survival knife? Well, in the eighth grade anything can happen. You could end up lost and have to chop down a bunch of trees and build a log cabin for the night, you could be attacked by rabid beavers, or in the worst case scenario, the Soviet Union could've finally made their move and invaded and we would've had to go all *Wolverines!* on them.

159

In the eighth grade a big ass survival knife was the answer to just about everything. If you were going out into the woods, or the back yard for that matter, you had the big ass survival knife. Plus, there was that extra bit of fishing line and a couple hooks in the handle. So technically it was fishing gear.

I caught a lot of fish back then. Lots of bass. And bluegills, and bull head. And bull frogs for that matter. It was a different kind of fishing but yet it was still the same. It was about going out and proving that you could outsmart an animal that had a brain the size of the tip of your pinky finger. It was about leaving your parents back at the house and doing something on your own, no supervision. It was about not caring what the popular kids at school were wearing. It was about doing what *you* wanted to do and no one telling you that you were doing it wrong.

When you got skunked, you lied and said you caught a couple. When you had a good day in the woods on the side of that lake behind the no trespassing signs you felt like you owned the place, like the world was your urinal, piss on everyone who thought you'd never amount to much. Out there you were you, there was no show to put on, no speeches to be heard, and no one to tell you that the teeth on the back side of that survival knife were just about useless. You'd figure that out on your own and just like lying about fishing, you'd swear later on that you cut down four trees ten inches across with them to make a bridge to get across the mouth of the creek feeding the lake.

Some things don't change. Fishing is still my way to break away, to battle animals with little brains, except they seem to win more these days, or maybe I didn't really catch as many as I remember back then. *The older I get, the better I was* syndrome I like to call it. It's still about no supervision. Leaving *the man* behind, not punching a time clock, not taking direction from someone who doesn't know me for anything other than another number in the company. It's still about not giving a crap about the popular kids. Whatever the latest reality show is, making some moron famous for no other reason than being pretty, and pretty stupid, you can keep it. And it's still about doing it *my way.* These days it's with a fly rod instead of a spinning rod, but it's all about doing *my* thing.

All the Facebook banter on the fly pages about "you're doing it wrong" is left right there on the internet when I hit the water. Reading some of the "you're doing it wrong" comments turns Facebook into "facepalmbook" for me because there's no rules other than your local laws and your good conscience. There's no right or wrong way to do this. There's a right way for people to breath, and that's above water, because we don't have gills. There's a right way for people to eat and drink, and that's by putting it in your mouth, because it won't get where it needs to by shoving it in any other orifice, and even if it could, some people's heads would be blocking the way. But there's no right way to fly fish. You have a fly rod, you have a fly reel, and the rest is up to you. Where, when, and with what is *your* way.

The only thing that's changed for me is there's no big ass survival knife on my side when I go out anymore. I'll burry myself in a pile of leaves if I get lost overnight (the only thing I do more than get lost is fall in rivers). I carry so much gear now that the little bit of line and the couple hooks in the handle would be trivial at best, and fly line would most definitely get tangled around the handle at the worst times. So no, there's no big ass survival knife on my side anymore. I leave it in the Jeep. Because, you never know when you may have to build a bridge to drive out.

The Old Man Said So

When I was a cell tower climber 95 percent of the time we were out somewhere on the countryside, in the hills, up on mountains, our days full of long drives, great views, and I usually ended them fishing somewhere far from home. But there was always that 5 percent when the drive wasn't far, and the view was nothing more than looking at other rooftops from the rooftop your job was on. Nothing to write home about, and no fishing to be had at the end of the day.

On one such job, myself and one other guy, my buddy Mike Street who I'd spent equally as much time on the towers with and on the water with afterwards were doing a small antenna job on a roof top in Syracuse. Below us were five floors of antique shop, which to me means old pocket knives and fishing gear. Getting our tools and equipment to the roof required a ride in the buildings old freight elevator, operated by an older gentleman that reminded me of the late George Burns. He had the mannerisms, the style, and the charisma of a generation on its way out of the world, one being replaced by a bunch of rude and entitlement expecting lazy people.

At one point while Mike was out in the truck going over paperwork on the phone with someone back at the shop I seized the moment to search the first floor for the antique fishing booty I knew could be found if I looked, and sure enough my hunt turned up one shelf with a couple old sailing ship models, and scattered about them were several old reels, one of them being one of those old quirky automatic fly reels. A dark green trimmed in white, Horrocks-Ibbotson. Not only was it cool, and made in the city in which I was born, but it was only 14 bucks. I had to have it.

As the elevator climbed, I asked the old man what time they closed up, so that we could be sure to be done with the job and packed up with a few minutes to spare so that I could make my purchase. I then laughed and said "My wife is going to kill me. We just had the discussion that I've got more than enough old fishing stuff on my walls and that I should stop bringing stuff home. Maybe I should leave it where I found it." Mike chuckled, but George Burns stood with his hand on the sliding elevator door frame and looked me in the eyes. He looked at the harness over my shoulder and the lineman's bags full of tools at our feet and then he spoke.

"Do you work hard?" I nodded and answered "Yep." "Do you pay your bills?" Again I answered "Yep." Do you run around on your wife?" "No sir." He looked at Mike and then back to me, "So you work hard and you don't cheat on your wife?" "That's right." He nodded in approval and then told me "Buy the damn reel. It's only 14 dollars." Mike laughed and I grinned. He was right, or a really good salesman. Or both.

A week later my father was over to the house and we were out in my room filled with fishing paraphernalia, Holly doing something on the computer for him as we talked about where the hot fishing spot was for the week. He spotted the auto reel on the wall and pointed to it and said "Hey, I just bought one of these from an antique shop a few weeks ago, just a different color!" I told him I'd found it at the shop in Syracuse and Holly looked up at me with that *Oh really,...I thought we had an understanding* look on her face. I had to come up with something to legitimize the purchase fast so I relayed the old man's wisdom as fast and to the point as I could.

"Listen. This old guy that looked like George Burns told me to buy the reel or cheat on you. I think I made the right decision!" That was two years ago. I'm still adding old gear to the wall whenever I find it.

Backstage Passes

Winter never really showed up this year, but for some reason spring wouldn't either. We've been stuck in that weird, in between twilight zone where the temperatures hover right on the edge of snow and rain. When we'd get snow, the ground was too warm for it to stick, and when we'd get rain, it was cold and damp like a late fall day, and the lack of any leaves or green ground cover only intensified the feeling during those days that this was still not spring, even though winter was done with. And then almost out of nowhere this past weekend spring arrived like a rock star strolling down the red carpet. "Everyone look at me, I'm awesome, and I'm who you wish you could be."

Holly told me to go fishing. When your wife says go, you go. So I went. I flirted with the idea of heading north like usual and hitting a brook trout stream, like usual. But the sun was so warm on my face, the sky so blue, it felt like we'd almost skipped spring and moved right into summer. And to me summer means bass. I had bass on my mind. After a long, odd winter dreaming of not much more than chasing brookies in the spring, only interrupted by a quick foray to Florida salt water, I was abruptly skipping over trout, rushing past the opening of walleye and pike, and diving straight into Bass. I'd waited six months for brookies, only to then want to skip ahead two more for bass. It's true, humans can never be happy with what they have.

Like a left hook out of nowhere I was on my way to a still water with the canoe strapped to the roof and a 7wt rigged with a heavy leader and a streamer. If spring was the rock star, then the anglers were the concert goers. And Delta Lake was the venue. Pulling the Jeep to the shoulder of the road was like pulling into the parking lot at the concert, all that was missing was the ticket line. Cars and trucks lined the shoulder, fisherman lined the road side shore line, and boats bobbed and weaved on the water, scattered, moving in all directions. Like ants swarming over a giant chocolate chip cookie left on the sidewalk, not knowing where to begin the feast, but wanting to get it all at once.

It took me about two hours of paddling, trolling, casting streamers both to structure and blindly to open water, and just sitting, bobbing in the wake of the plethora of bass boats cruising the pea green tinted

164

water to figure out that I should move on. This was just not to be today.

Most of the concert goers had figured it out too, that the rock star had turned out to be Axl Rose, coming in with a long, shrieking wail, but ending up being just another washed up celebrity who took himself way to seriously. Returning to the shore, I saw that only a handful of trucks remained, the diehards who refused to believe that Guns-N-Roses wouldn't make a comeback. Me, I'd come to terms, I was ready to move on. I heard that Tom Petty was playing down on the Mohawk River right around the corner from the house. And Tom Petty never gets old.

Pulling into the lot sandwiched between the Mohawk River and the Barge Canal, I was greeted yet again by concert goers. I pulled into the last open parking spot. Apparently I wasn't the only one who knew Tom Petty could still hold a tune. As I pocketed my fly box and inspected the 7wt I suddenly remembered the glass 5wt in the rod tube on the roof and thought to myself, glass seemed more "Tom Petty" speed. It was smooth and packed a lot of power and emotion, without being as over bearing and brutish as the 7wt. I stowed the 7wt back in the Jeep and removed the glass rod. I looked over my surroundings.

Right was the path to the canal. I could already see from here the lawn chairs and fishing rods propped in the crotches of sticks poked into the ground. Left was the path to the Mohawk, the grass path had been beaten to a muddy pulp from the hordes of partiers looking for the beer tent, and straight was woods, then a field, then more woods, and somewhere in there was the Mohawk River. Upstream and away from the parking lot, from the easy access foot paths. The back stage pass.

I made my way through a tree line, a field where I stopped and paused as gun shots rang out while three young men tossed clay targets into the air and blasted them, and then into another tree line. The river wasn't far, and before I knew it I was surveying the flows, inspecting shadows, deciphering what were logs and rocks and what might be fish, hoping that I'd spot them before they spotted me. Hoping my intrusion back stage wouldn't be found out until I'd gotten to meet Tom Petty or at least had a glimpse close up.

It wasn't long before I spotted movement in fish form. Three smallmouth hung just up in the mouth of a very small stream feeding into the river, and I crouched on dry leaves above the muddy bank side an easy eight feet above them, trying to figure out how to make a cast from such an odd angle within a stand of close trees, and what I would do if I actually hooked one and had to get down to the water. The last part was easy, I'd do what I had to do to shake Tom Petty's hand back stage. I'd slide down that muddy bank like a skate boarder owning the half pipe and stop just inches short of getting wet. I'd worry about getting back up after the deed was done.

The black Woolly Bugger drifted right past all three bass not once but three times. Dead drift, a slight twitch, an all-out fast strip break for freedom. The three amigos guarding the mouth of the stream inspected my imitation, and called my bluff. On the fourth attempt I let it pass them by without hardly a glance and continue into the main river where I thought I had snagged a branch or something unseen in the slightly deeper and hazing water where the stream and river mixed. And then the line tightened and moved downstream. Hello Tom Petty, nice to meet you. It was so worth the effort of sneaking back stage. You should try it some time, I highly recommend it.

Fly Fishing in the Blood

Everyone has that one fishing place that trumps all others. Mine's a small lake surrounded by rolling farm lands and a small green hump of a mountain on a farm that belongs to distant cousins in Cobleskill NY. My grandfather started picking me up before sunrise on Sundays sometime around the second grade to drive the hour and a half in a pickup, over weighted with the tools of a crack mechanic that smelled of gear oil and cigarettes, so that we could sit in the grass and drown worms all day.

We did this my entire youth, all the way up until I left for the Air Force after high school. We hardly spoke at all. He was one of my best friends truth be told but I have a very hard time remembering his voice, we spoke so little. But I can hear his gruff, raspy, smokers laugh as I'd complain that the sunfish had stolen my worm again like it just happened yesterday. It wasn't until I stood in the barn four years ago, talking to Wanda, our distant cousin, daughter off my great great aunt that I found the motivation to actually learn to use the fly rod that my father had bought me that spring.

Standing there in the old broken barn, the smells and sounds of a dairy farm surrounding us, and having my oldest son Jacob with me, we talked about how Jake was the fifth generation of the Usyk family to fish this spot, starting with my great grandfather, Wanda's uncle. I knew he'd brought his grandchildren here, just like my grandfather had brought his, but out of nowhere came a piece of information I'd yet to learn. My great grandfather was a fly fisherman, and he'd cast a fly rod on this very lake. Where frustration had hampered my will to learn the fly rod up to this point, after learning of my great grandfather, and the deep connection that I have with the farm lake, I told myself right then and there I'd learn the fly rod and fish this lake with it if it was the last thing I ever did.

Two years later, on my yearly pilgrimage to the farm, I found myself sitting in the canoe with Jake, a fly rod in my hand, my great grandfather's blood pumping through my veins, from my heart, down my arm, and to the very fingers which held the cork handle as the rod bent on the back cast. The same blood, enabling the same grasp of cork, creating the same bend of a fly rod. I can tell you I know when something feels right because of that experience if nothing else.

I'd tied streamers for the most part for this outing, and had only one frog popper. We sat in the canoe off a weed bed on the right bank. And there was a splash. And another. And before long, in a matter of ten minutes, bass could be found to be breaking the surface in almost all directions. My streamers went ignored, the feast was taking place as Mother Nature served up a platter of dragon and damsel flies unlike which I'd never seen. They darted everywhere, hovering a foot above the water, weaving, bobbing, dipping to the surface to cause a tiny ring and miniscule splash, only to lift off again, to race off before death from below snatched them up in crushing jaws.

I had no dragon fly patterns, nothing even remotely close. Panic almost overtook me. Matching the hatch was possibly the most important aspect of fly fishing, and I had failed miserably in my preparations for the trip. What could I do? I looked at the popper. A frog? What did I have to lose? It was at least a top water fly if nothing else.

The wind resistant foam body and plume of feathers growing from its butt proved a challenge for me to cast much more than twenty-five feet at first, but that was all it took. Upon the dull slap of its landing, the water opened as if a toilet was being flushed beneath it and the popper was gone! The most perfect twelve inch largemouth came to the side of the canoe and I smiled. Cast after cast, the bass hammered and crushed, leaping from the water as if to give us a show. They were so keyed in on anything that moved above the water that I swear they were watching my fly pass above on the false cast before touch down on the final forward cast and then pouncing as the first fiber of feather made contact with the water's surface. I swear, so intent on the movement above, that one bass actually launched itself fully from the water and took the popper out of midair. It was like watching great whites destroy sea lions during Shark Week.

It was the perfect day, and in a roundabout way, one that was prompted years before I was ever even thought of, by a man that I never got to fish with. Well, not until that day. On that day, with my

Father being on the water too, and Jacob as well, I believe all five generations were there. I don't think I was the only one swinging a fly rod either, because there were fish jumping at something I just couldn't see now and then. We were all there.

The One That Got Away

It wasn't as hot and humid as the weather man had predicted. It was overcast and maybe 72. The water flowed a clear tinted tea color, as most Adirondack streams and rivers do, unlike the waters back home. 72 miles south, the creek that flowed past my house was a far from translucent dark brown, the color of liquid mud from days of rain and run off. We waded up stream, myself lost in the beauty and serenity of a remote stream that I'd fished only a few times before, yet I felt I knew it well. I was glad the water back home was blown out in all honesty, it was the perfect excuse for me to suggest to my fishing buddy Brian, that we should make the 70 mile drive to clearer water, my last convincing sentence, the deal closer, being "I've never been skunked there before." What fisherman in his right mind would choose any other place?

It was almost perfect. The only reason for swearing, was also the reason for keeping your mouth closed. If there's irony, it'll usually find me and slap me in the face, or in this case, bite me in the face. And on the fingers, the knuckles to be exact. And even though we wore long sleeves doused in deet, and I even pulled a hood up over my head, the Adirondack black flies and mosquitos bit through clothing, the sting and the itch felt on my back the proof.

Everyone thinks that where *they* come from they've got the worst mosquitos, the most vicious biting insects. Well, I can tell you right now that I believe the Adirondack black flies and mosquitos, just like the Adirondack Park itself could swallow up all the other great parks in our country, its black flies and mosquitos could swallow up their winged warriors hands down. I swear that the black flies were elbowing the mosquitos out of the way to get to us and vice versa, like starving Ethiopians dropped at a Golden Corral buffet, they fought for every inch and feasted like they'd never eaten before. The bites on my hands a day later tells me they ate well.

I once saw a short film about some fly fisherman making a first decent of an unnamed river up in Alaska, and at one point in their portaging of gear they were shown to be covered in mosquitos to the point that they couldn't even talk. So I figure Alaska could give our black flies a run for their money, but I've never understood why you'd want to brag about how something you have is the *worst*.

But the bugs weren't the only things biting. Brian had caught a nice smallmouth where the small stream cascaded down over shelves of bed rock into bigger waters at the start and now we were into brookie territory above that. Now as we traveled up stream, hopping rock to rock and skirting along the edge on a marked trail that more resembled an animal path in most places, the wild brook trout that called the stream home would dart out from pocket water or dark pools to chase a white streamer. Their colors were magnificent, their markings second to none. Several times the thought entered my mind that if the fish were what I was chasing, then perhaps it was partly because of where I had to go to chase them. The places I found them in were as beautiful as the fish themselves.

And then there was the hole. 75 yards upstream of a huge boulder that spanned nearly the entire width of the stream, forcing the waters to narrow and cut out the far bank to pass, I found myself standing on the protruding rock that gave me a good upstream view, looking slightly down on what I didn't realize the first few times fishing here was a channel. A *deep* channel. Where most of this small stream was waist deep or much less, this channel could've possibly been over my head easily.

I didn't realize this until, as I cast my streamer into the white water at its head, rolling off rocks and becoming deep and dark, I stripped fast to try and over take the speed of the current to get my fly to move erratically. Ten feet above my position it shot up from the bottom. I was used to seeing the typical flashes of fish in the 6" to 10" size. The typical size of wild Adirondack brookie in these small streams. It shot up, it smashed the streamer, it rolled to turn back for the bottom, and I hollered. "BAM!" My 3wt doubled over and then almost immediately went slack. "AHHHHHHHHH!" A missed hook set.

I knew the odds of a second strike were slim, so I didn't waste time. I lifted the line from the water and as the rod loaded up on the first back cast I shot the streamer straight back to the white water and repeated the strip. The fish shot up again and gave an encore performance of its first, only this time it refused to touch the streamer, missing it by what looked like an inch or less. The dreaded trout refusal.

I yanked the line from the water and shot the streamer upstream a third time, stripping line frantically, my heart pounding and my hope fading, and the third time the fish rose again from the bottom, but didn't come nearly as close to the streamer before returning to the dark and out of site. A fourth cast was what I knew it would be. Pointless. As was the fifth, sixth, seventh, eighth, ninth, tenth, and however many more casts and countless strips of the line I made in desperation.

I don't catch big fish. It's never bothered me because I've never chased big fish, I've always been happy just to have a cork handle in my hand and the bend of the rod during the cast. The size of the fish has never been a deal breaker for me. As a matter of fact, I told someone once that I hoped I'd never catch a truly large fish. That I hoped the once in a life time catches went to other anglers, because honestly, catching a truly great fish might ruin all the other average fish from that point forward.

I enjoyed the rest of the day. I did. I was very happy with the brookies I caught afterwards. I was. But I keep seeing that fish come up from the bottom of a channel I didn't grasp was even there until it was too late. Easily a one pound fish in a stream where it's brothers and sisters all measure in ounces. I know I'll revisit this stream again. I will. But I'll have to fight the urge to run ahead upstream, to skip all the great spots downstream, to rush and get to the spot. That hidden channel. I'm afraid that fish may have ruined the entire stretch of stream for me and I didn't even catch it! It may have been ruined, not by my biggest catch on the stream...But by the one that got away.

Two weeks later JP texted me a picture after fishing the same stretch. A head on shot of a handful of fish, silver with spots. I texted back questioning, *is that a brown?* The idea of browns in the stream stocked over wild brook trout scared the hell out of me immediately. He sent a two word answer back. *Land Locked.* All I could say was a four letter word and kept thinking about that fish refusing to take my streamer. Son of a...

The Hole

I'd been up this stretch of small Adirondack stream before. It's the beginnings of one of the well-known rivers that flows from the largest park in the U.S. It makes its way out of the park and eventually empties into Lake Ontario., gaining volume and width along the way, the scenery changing many times over but always remaining rocky whether it be the river bottom or the banks it cuts through. I've fished it in so many places along its length that I feel I've fished the whole thing, but in reality I've fished less than one percent of the water.

It's here, in its early youthful stages that I enjoy it the most. Here I can hop from rock to rock, boulder to boulder, casting to pocket water as I pick my way up stream and pluck out the small but vibrant wild brook trout that call it home. I've fished upstream from here, and I've fished downstream, but there's still a stretch in between, a length that I'm not sure on its distance other than it would be a good long hike, that I've yet to discover in its entirety. The best thing to do would be to put my pup tent on my back and park the truck for a couple days and see what I see until I connect with familiar water from one end or the other, but for now, with an unpredictable work schedule, a wife, and kids who seem to find a way to play baseball through all four seasons of the year, I have to be satisfied with pushing just a little further on each visit.

So it was on this last visit that once again, I pushed just a little farther upstream. It's been a dry summer, and water levels are down everywhere. This makes traveling upstream on a rocky small stream that much easier, as there's more paths to choose, more dry rocks that I could use to cross from side to side. Even though water levels are down and the lakes feel like bath water, a small Adirondack stream like this one traveling in the shade of the trees *can* keep its cool temperatures. *But* you should always check the water temperatures out first in the heat of the summer.

When brook trout waters get above sixty-eight degrees the fish begin to get stressed and even if you *are* releasing them, the fight and the lactic acid they've built up in the heat will kill them. So I'm always careful not to fish for brookies in the hot summers unless I know they're still living in the cool comforts of home, the higher volume of rocks breaking the current actually makes their environment even more oxygen rich in many places, giving them a little more help. This is why the Adirondack brook trout is such a hardy fish, as delicate as trout may be. They thrive in the long and harsh conditions of the Adirondack winters and tough out the hot summers alike, as long as we anglers leave them be in the hard times.

I pushed upstream a little farther. There was a split, water poured over and through natural rocky impoundments on either side of a thin island of green pines and emptied into shallow pools on either side. Out of each pool I brought a colorful and energetic brookie to hand, before picking a side to continue up stream on. I stood back and thought in my head. "Choose your adventure." I went left. After a couple casts to pockets and another nice fish of average size, it came into view.

"It" being the one phrase that has been used to describe fishing spots most likely since the dawn of time, since the first spear was launched from the hands of the first man to come up with the idea, used in stories and songs too numerous to count, to be used by young and old anglers alike. "It" referring to the proverbial "fishing hole". The discovery of it stirred such emotions in me at that moment that I went from staring questionably as to if it was truly as it presented itself to next almost nearly falling in headfirst while hurrying upstream to get a closer look.

Indeed it was a great hole. On a stream where the current was considered to be deep if it reached your waist and where you could cross nearly anywhere by merely stepping from stone to stone, here were nine or ten boulders the size of small cars arranged in a circle, the stream above it either flowing off to its left and continuing on its typical path of scattered trout mountain goat country, or, as if planned perfectly by some higher powers, being forced through an opening between two massive boulders separated by about three feet, where it churned into the hole, calmed down and flowed deeply enough so that I could only make out the shapes of a couple large rocks in the deep bottom and then was forced back out the bottom end where it continued its trip down a maze of more boulders and blown down trees on the other side of the thin green island.

Even more amazingly was the placement of a shallow and mostly still pocket of water on its left flank, the very spot I'd been directed to by my original choice to take the left side past the spilt downstream some fifty yards. You could fish this hole from anywhere you liked, but I'd come to the best and most perfect spot. I could stay back, stay low, and cast to every inch of it.

I sent my small gray and white streamer flying to the water churning into the entrance and stripped through the small piece of white water. As it cleared the commotion and entered the edge of the calmer flow, there was a flash of dark and pinkish belly as the water absolutely exploded. There was no tug, the fish had missed it completely. I kept stripping slowly hoping it would follow and hit again, but nothing.

I cast again to the same spot, and once again in the exact same spot came the explosion, the slashing at the fly, and once again nothing on the hook, not even the chance at a hook set. I paused. Should I let the fish be or take the chance of giving it lock jaw and shutting down the entire hole with another cast to the same spot?

The hope at the end of the cast got the better of me and I repeated the cast again. The streamer cleared the fast water, the fish launched, the line bumped, and once again I had nothing to show for it. What was this fish doing? He attacked my fly three times as if he wanted to kill it, like a mugger leaping from a dark alley but missing the purse altogether, and he tried it three times in a row! Could he possibly try it a forth or would the jig finally be up? There was only one way to find out.

I cast. The streamer smacked down at the edge of the churning and boiling water, I stripped twice. The flash of belly was there again, only this time it didn't break the surface of the water. This time the line went tight, the 3wt bent and danced, and the fish fought to return to its ambush position as I fought to bring it to me as quickly as possible. I didn't want it getting out into the hole and causing a commotion that would scare off any other possible takers, and I didn't want to lose it. Surely if it got off this time, there'd be no fifth chance. This was it.

The fish was less colorful than all the previous catches on my way upstream, but nearly twice their size. I smiled. I talked to myself out loud. I talked to the fish as I removed the hook. I thanked it for a game well played, and watched it regain its composure and its breath on the bottom of the slack water I stood in before it glided back into the hole and disappeared. Then I cast to another spot on the other side and the scenario played out almost the same once again with the second fish of about equal size.

In a land of seven inch fish, twelve inches is a giant. And in a land void of human voices, the sounds of traffic, or the smell of anything besides the great pines and the fresh clean water, there's never a bad day. To find a "fishing hole" in such a place is truly a remarkable thing, the thing on which memories are made and legends of *the spot*, *the hole* that someone knows grow from. I don't keep secret fishing spots. I'm just not that kind of guy. I'll tell you where I fish, have at it, just carry your trash out and be nice to the things that swim there.

Well, except this place. Ask me where this place is. I didn't tell you? Must not be any of your business! Go find your own darn hole! But I'll give you a hint. If you haven't found it yet...You need to go a little farther.

Life Lessons on the Fly

We stood on the bridge, looking down to the small stream and the fly fisherman standing knee deep in the soft current. The sun had been up for a couple hours now, and birds flitted here and there in the trees. The swallows that are built for speed would come zooming down the stream weaving and swooping, looking as if they were having fun while getting their fill of the morning insects. Truth be told they probably do. It's hard to say if a bird is smiling as it passes by at fifty miles an hour but it probably is.

The insects have such a tough life. Death from above and from below. Swooping birds and rising trout. And then there are the humans, constantly swatting and squashing and spraying poisons. It's no wonder the bugs spend years of their lives under rocks on the bottoms of streams only to hatch and fly for merely a day or less before dying. We consider them thoughtless things, but maybe there's more to learn from them than we think after all.

The angler was casting up stream and across, tight loops in the air and a dry fly that couldn't be registered by the human eye from this distance resting on a current, carrying it towards a decent sized rock mid-stream. Beyond the rock, between it and the scrubby far bank,   I pointed out the light splashes to my son. The trout taking insects from the surface. There looked to be two or three of them working close to the bank but the angler couldn't seem to find the right trajectory to land his dry fly and then mend his line to get the perfect drift, the drift that would fool the fish.

My son's voice raised from a whisper to an elevated and excited one as he saw three good rises all about the same time. Then we saw the rise of the fish that was in front of the rock, less than twenty feet from the angler. The angler adjusted his footing on the gravel bottom, twisted his torso and lifted the line off the water and with one fluid movement shot fly line, leader, and dry fly forward and upstream of the spot the fish rose last.

From our perch on the bridge we couldn't tell still where the dry fly was, but when the fish rose again in the same spot and the angler hadn't lifted his rod tip we knew that the trick had failed. With the lift of the rod the line was once again shot forward and upstream for another drift through the feeding trout's water, and two more times the fish splashed but the line didn't go tight.

Now whether these were last second refusals of the fly or absolute indifference to it, the fish taking the real deal somewhere close in proximity we couldn't tell, but I explained to Jacob how a trout will sometimes rise to a fisherman's fly only to taunt them but never actually take the fake. That a trout, as small of a brain as they have, has an instinct engrained in it over thousands of years that tells it somehow that something isn't right. Sometimes you can find the fault in the drag of the fly line across a different current pulling the fly unnaturally on top, sometimes you can blame the pattern for being the wrong one, the wrong color, maybe the wrong size, and sometimes it's just a fish that won't fall for it.

I've got to believe that fly fishing has a lot to teach. That in today's world where every kid gets a trophy, and every kid makes the team, fly fishing can teach the lessons of losing better than many other things that kill time and bring parents and children together. In fly fishing, there's a needed focus to both master the cast and to understand the situation at hand. And the fact that you could have everything perfect, just so, and still fail is a lesson that too many people deny our youth today. Some days it's just not going to come together, it's just not going to end in your favor, and you have to deal with it. It's not that you didn't try hard enough, you just got beat. You have to keep casting, like a little leaguer in a slump of losses you just have to keep swinging for the fence.

After about five or six casts there was a splash, and the angler lifted his rod. The rod bent and danced a happy dance, and a small wild brook trout swam circles in front of the fisherman as he brought it in closer and closer. We crashed down the bank from the bridge and my son got a good look at the fish just as it was being released, his smile as big as the man who'd just done the catching. And there's the final lesson.

No matter how much of a slump you may be in, no matter how the odds may be stacked against you, and no matter how many times you might fail, eventually you'll find yourself with a fish in hand, or with a baseball sailing through the air following the crack of the bat. I think if more kids fished, life would become clearer earlier on. You can't win them all. But that's no reason not to make the cast. In fly fishing not everyone gets a trophy. You just keep casting.

Family Camping Trips Aren't Fishing Trips

Every summer we go on a camping trip with another family. It's been going on a for a few years now, and when we get to planning it in early spring my only input besides that it needs to be someplace we haven't been yet would of course be that there should be water. Kids need water to keep them busy, and so do I. I think we all know where this is going but let me be clear here. A family camping trip is not a fishing trip. It's a family camping trip.

The Jeep gets a huge, gigantic ten person tent, a pile of camp chairs, and a canoe strapped down up top. Inside there's a big cooler, a large beach bag full of all the beachy stuff, a couple backpacks stuffed to the brink and threatening to explode, bags of snacks, toys, more clothes, four sleeping bags, an *air mattress,* three pillows... Listen. That's one pillow for Holly and one for each of the boys. Three because the non-use of a pillow while camping is my final hold out to how I believe camping should be done as opposed to how it's now done with the huge tent and all that previously listed crap... If we have to stay at state campgrounds with bathrooms and showers then damn it, I'm not using a pillow. It's all that's left to *roughing it,* and I'm holding onto it like a three year old holds on to their blankie. You'll have to knock me out with some type of narcotic in my beer and then slide a pillow under my thick skull while I'm in a coma to get me to use a *pillow*, just like the A-Team used to have to do to Mr. T to get him on a plane back in the good old days.

Anyways, in short, there's no room left after you pack the Jeep for a family camping trip for a bunch of fly fishing gear. Which is why I only bring two fly rods. Ok, maybe three. But one's always on the roof in the rod tube anyhow, so it doesn't really count. It's a part of the Jeep like the spare tire. But it's *not* a fishing trip.

Normally, because it's not a fishing trip, I reserve my fishing time to the crack of dawn while everyone else is still sleeping in the main lodge room of our overly huge tent, the wife on the *air mattress,* and the boys on their foam pads. But the past couple years I've also just about thrown my right shoulder out casting poppers like a mad man in the last half hour of sunlight. The fish bite possibly the best then, and casting into a sunset makes for a memorable experience, but let's be honest. Kids.

The kids have tried to behave all day. But by this time, not only are we all tired of yelling at them that baseball bats aren't part of hide and seek or to quit chasing the freak'n ducks, but they're pretty much on behaving overload as well, and we've found that if you want them to go to sleep you just have to let them run around through the trees like little savages, the neighboring campsites flipping over picnic tables to use as cover and throwing more wood on their fires because we all know fire keeps animals at bay. Unless of course those animals have marshmallows on the ends of pointy sticks in which case the fire attracts them like moths who want nothing more than to ignite the sugary napalm on a stick invention and wave it around like they're trying to signal a plane to land, or look like an out of practice flaming baton twirler at the circus.

This can all be handled calmly from a distance. Like, standing in a canoe in the middle of the lake casting a fly rod while the high pitched screams of a little girl and the blood curdling war cries of three little boys echo across the entire central region of the Adirondacks type distance. But I digress.

This last trip we stayed on Lake Durant, with a stunning view of Blue Mountain across the lake from our site. We got there and set up camp late Friday afternoon, and Saturday morning I stealthily rolled off the *air mattress* and grabbed the rolled up shirt I had used as a pillow and snuck out. Both the boys sleep on sleeping pads on the opposite end of the great hall and were, as usual, mostly off the pads, the sleeping bags twisted around their legs and their bodies in a semi-fetal position trying to stay warm and most likely uncomfortably sleeping on jutting tree roots under the tent floor. I never attempt to push them back onto the pads, because it's common camping knowledge that it's not true camping without a little discomfort, without a crink in your neck or a sore back from sleeping on rocks and roots. Holly was fast asleep on the *air mattress.* I never mess with her, because, it's also common camping knowledge not to mess with mama bear.

That morning on the lake there was a heavy fog rolling through, every now and then the very top of Blue Mountain showed its self above the fog, but only as a black shape, there was no detail. A fuzzy black hump poking through the fog high above the lake. I gave the 7wt a workout casting a popper to every lily pad on our side of the lake and to the water surrounding every boulder that protruded from the lake's surface, but other than a couple tiny pan fish that would pull it under but probably weren't big enough to take it, there was no fish activity anywhere.

The couple motor boats that left the boat launch and headed straight to the opposite end of the lake came back in an hour or less which told me the fish must not have been biting on that end either. The lake holds largemouth bass but it's stocked with tiger muskies as well, and I could tell from the size of the lures hanging off the ends of the fishing poles standing in rod holders that the toothy fish were what they were after. Me, I'd have been happy with a bluegill or two. The morning was a skunk, but it was quiet and peaceful out there and the fog had burned off by the time the canoe bumped the shore back at the site. I could smell bacon cooking over the camp fire, so it was shaping up to be a good day. Because, you know, bacon.

Sometime after lunch a walk down to the beach was being organized, and I saw this as another opportunity to fish, because I'm not much of a beach person, and on these camping trips if I'm not fishing then I need to have a beer in my hand. But there's no bottles allowed at the beach so I *had* to go fishing. I don't see the point of sitting in the sand staring at the water when you could be catching fish in the same water. I'd also been told by someone a few days before that the creek flowing out of the lake was a good creek for bass, and the beach area just happened to be a couple hundred yards from the creek. All the signs pointed to the creek and a fly rod.

So as kids were changing into bathing suits and towels and snacks were being packed in bags I asked Jacob and Carter if they wanted to go fishing while we were down there since it was close. Jacob said "Nah, I just want to swim" but Carter jumped all over it. Jake is the older of the two, and while he *will* fish, you have to catch him at the right time, when he's in the right mood. I never push the subject when he doesn't want to because my parents insisted that I played soccer when I was a little kid about Carter's age and I hated it. Actually I didn't really like it, but once I was forced to play, then I hated it. So I let Jake fish on his own terms. Carter on the other hand usually asks me to take him before I can ask.

So when we got to the beach Carter and I kept walking while the others split off. I had my fly rod and a small chest pack full of flies and tippets and a small container full of marabou jigs for Carter to fish on his ultralight spin cast rod, which was firmly grasped in his right hand held upright as if he were carrying a flag in a parade.

At the boat launch just above the dam there were four guys with beards and tattoos chucking big Rapalas out about a hundred feet and cranking them back, beer cans littered the ground around their tackle boxes. I nodded and we slipped off around some bushes and trees and made our way down below the small dam.

The creek started as a small water fall running over the dam and crashing down about fifteen feet and then rushing over a small concrete shelf into a pool. The pool wasn't more than twenty feet long give or take and the tail out looked like the perfect place to send a 6yr old out to wade and toss a jig into the head where the white water frothed and churned. There was no way he wouldn't catch something here. It might not be a monster, but 6yr olds don't need monsters, they just need slimy little wiggly fish to be happy. The spot looked so fishy that I figured the only place you were more likely to find fish was in a catholic town on a Friday night during lent.

Sure enough, after only wading over to the side and removing his jig from the trees twice for him, on one of his first well placed casts, right into the white water, and after telling him to reel faster to keep it from snagging on the bottom, his little rod bent over and he turned to look back at me over his shoulder with a little astonishment in his eyes. No matter how many fish this kid catches, the first one of the day always comes as a surprise to him as if he didn't think it was possible to do. I laughed and half yelled "reel it in!" and managed to get to him with my net as he just about ran out of line to reel. I handed him the net and he looked at me like I was nuts, but I shoved it into his hand and told him to point the rod high to get the fish closer and then scoop it up.

It was a tiny smallmouth, probably no more than eight inches long. It may as well have been four feet long and a hundred pounds as he stood there with the rod in one hand and the netted fish in the other and a grin the size of the Grand Canyon. The funniest part was after he released it, after two more casts, he turned to me again and this time he says it can be my turn to fish. He can't use up the spot all for himself, he has to let me fish a little.

Carter, the triumphant 6yr old, was the only one to catch a fish from that pool. After he went to the beach with the others I waded downstream a little ways and in what looked like prime smallmouth water managed to catch a handful of bluegills, but that was it. And I do mean handful. And I've got small hands. Carter caught the biggest fish of the afternoon. And trust me, if you've never been out fished by a 6yr old, it's not so bad.

I'd love to tell you that later that evening on our last night there I landed a whopper of a large mouth or that the canoe was attacked by a tiger muskie with some legendary name that was talked about in stories by the fishermen at the local bait shop, but all I did was paddle out to the middle of the lake and cover about five square miles of water to come up with one ten inch largemouth and one about fourteen or so, while the echoes of the yelling kids playing tag in the woods carried across the lake. But I cast like a mad man straight into the pink and

184

purple sun set like I might never cast a line again. If I made twenty casts I made a thousand.

Some kind of little house fly looking bugs swarmed the canoe and only bit from my ankles down, and I missed a couple strikes because I was leaning down and slapping like a hillbilly at a square dance, but all in all it's never the size of the fish or the number, it's the experience as a whole and the memories. Unless of course you catch a monster. *Then* it's about really big fish.

The Least I Can Do

It starts as several little branches, wandering through the Adirondacks like lost souls without a care. Some begin as the outflows of small ponds with no names in a boreal forest, some gather the trickles of streams that only flow in the spring as snow melts and gradually become larger streams, and yet others appear from the ground itself. These are the beginnings of an Adirondack water shed I'm only just beginning to get to know, yet feel as connected to as if I've known it my entire life.

These branches flow through dense, pathless, near impenetrable forest, and as they gather the miles they also gather width and depth, but still remain what you'd call a stream. They all finally become one just before entering a notable lake, and through this lake these waters pass, until it becomes the outlet of this fine lake which at the same point becomes the growing inlet of a greater lake some six miles downstream.

These waters hold wild brook trout, and it's because of these trout that I've spent so many days over the past two seasons hopping from rock to rock, crouching on the bank in the cover of green ferns, and exploring around each new bend, pushing farther upstream or down from either end, making it my goal to finally say that I've fished the entire thing, and this past week I could say that I have done just that.

That of course doesn't mean that I know the stream with any intimacy, although there are a couple runs I can say I know very well. I could never claim to know where all the deep holes are, or where the largest fish live, although the fishing can be so good that I've in fact only ever been skunked on it once, and that blame I lay on the storm the day before raising the water level to raging white waters on several runs.

In this stream, what I've learned is if it looks fishy you cast to it. There's probably going to be a flash of coppery pink, the tea color tinted waters playing on the pink belly of a brookie. If it doesn't look fishy, well, even then I've found many times the dart of a black fish shape and the same flash as a fish takes and turns.

This is nothing but a tiny pin point on the map of the Adirondack Park, yet to fish it and be totally honest with myself, I know I'll never discover all of its secrets. That doesn't mean I won't try, but to be honest again, I'm not sure that I want to. Somethings are greater with mystery, so I travel to this water shed not trying to pry answers from it, but more waiting to see what information it willing gives up.

This is not my stream. I think it's completely the opposite. The stream doesn't belong to me, I belong to the stream. And so I'll do what I can while sharing its space to protect it. I'll carry out what I carry in. I'll catch and release, I'll tread lightly and leave no trace. This is the least I can do for such a great friend that I've only just met. It's already done more for me than I could ever repay.

The Carp Incident

There's two fish that call my local waters home that I'd love to scratch off my list of fish caught on the fly that keep evading me. Let's cut right to the point. Carp and northern pike have been making me feel like the village idiot for a couple years now. Before you start making fun of me, it's not like I've been going out day after day for years chasing nothing but carp or pike and coming up empty handed, it's not like that at all. I spend a lot of time exploring Adirondack streams for brookies and bumming around creeks for smallmouths. It's more like when I'm out and there's carp or pike present and I give them a shot, well, that's when it all falls apart. That's when I hear fish laughing.

Two years ago I made it a goal to catch a northern on the fly rod. I've got so many streamers tied in every color, profile, and size with pike being the underlying motivation behind them that the inside of my big streamer box looks more like a hippies tie dyed t-shirt. But of course I keep gluing more crap to hooks *just in case* the next one might be the one to hook up.

But after missing and/or losing count of how many pike I've missed and/or lost, and after realizing that I was getting frustrated and angry on the water instead of relaxing and having a good time, I decided to quit targeting them specifically. I decided to just go fishing, and if I hooked one and got it to hand while bass fishing then so be it. But I wasn't about to let fly fishing become work with bad days and all. That's the whole point of it, to avoid that stuff altogether.

So while I've had follows, missed strikes, and a few breakoffs with pike, I've had even less contact with carp. Usually by the time I've spotted them they've spotted me, and while people seem to think that trout are the ultimate challenge, the most picky and fickle fish that swims in fresh water, I can tell you they've got nothing on carp. There they are. I cast. There they aren't.

I suck, or they're really good. I'd like to think that it's more that they're *that good* then that I suck, but then that's admitting that an animal with a little brain that a lot of anglers refer to as a garbage fish, a dirty bottom feeder, is smarter than me. Which is saying I suck. So either way, I guess I suck. Stupid fish. Oh wait. I've just surmised that they're *pretty smart*. But I digress.

I've tried them in a retention pond close to home, one that's usually a dingy brown, nothing to be seen but the tops of the weed beds and the dark shapes of fish with big heads tapering back to tails that sometimes come up out of the water while they root around for God knows what in the muck of the bottom, only to have my offerings ignored in full. And I've tried them on the lake, from my canoe and from the bow of JP's john boat as they rolled on the top, right there, close enough to make out individual scales as they scoffed at a lousy cast or a lousier fly before disappearing. I've dropped weighted leech patterns to them in the depths of the Barge Canal too, only to have them glide on by as if it wasn't even there.

I even happen to know of an old defunct and decrepit factory that has a large concrete pond full of them as well. The pond served as some type of either cooling pond or reservoir in case of fire when the factory produced guns for WWII, and later in its life the pond became a bit of a show piece with restaurant tables flanking it when the factory had a short life as an outlet mall, when I was in grade school. I can still remember looking down on the court yard as a child from an upper floor and seeing all the fish from above while people ate and talked all around them in their concrete banked ecosystem.

I know they're still in it, as I bought some equipment out of the building a few years ago and had to walk by the retaining pond. At first glance the pond water was nothing but a greenish brown liquid, with algae covering some of its surface looking like some kind of disintegrating carpet. But it only took standing at its edge for a mere few seconds before a huge scaled back and then tail passed by close enough to touch. The more I looked, the more huge fish I saw.

Of course last year I finally tracked down a friend of the owner of the property and expressed my interest in obtaining access, to which I was told *I'll see what I can do. There's actually a row boat in the pond these days.* I thought it would make for an absolutely great story, but in the end decided not to push the issue and let it go. My reasons were simple enough. If I ended up getting skunked in a manmade holding tank full of the damn things I'd most likely start questioning everything I thought I knew in life, and with witnesses, I'd probably never live it down.

So a few weeks ago while I was a jobless fish bum I ended up in the old canoe, drifting down the Mohawk River, casting my 7wt and decent sized streamers looking for smallmouths. I was striking out. I caught one smallmouth in about an hour, the only one I saw. There were however carp everywhere.

I should've switched to something smaller and "carp-ish" from the beginning when I first spotted five of them lingering in a deep pool in a bend of the river, all big, and all seemed to be on the search. My first clue should've been when I tossed a silver bait fish imitation to a shallow and stripped it to a drop off where I let it sink slowly to the bottom like a dead fish on its side. A massive carp with scales like armor out of a medieval tale hurried to within three feet of it before stopping and staring it down.

I didn't take it seriously because of my previous interactions with the lumbering brutes, I just laughed at it and talked to it like I talk to the family dog, as if it's really understanding me. "What, you're actually going to take a four inch streamer? Ha, yea sure you are." Then I twitched the streamer on the bottom and the Carp actually moved in closer. So I picked it up off the bottom with a tiny twitch, and the carp turned away. As I drifted past the bend I did wonder however if I could have taken the fish on that streamer. Maybe I should have just let it lie there on the bottom. It *did* seem interested at first.

I came to another dark and deep pool in another bend and as I stood in the boat, my calves braced against the portage bar of the canoe, thinking about how many times I was told when I was younger to never stand in a canoe, and there they were again. A whole bunch of big teardrop fish shapes, cruising up and down this small section of river, deep enough that I was seeing more silhouette than detail. But they were there, and there had to be half a dozen or more. I had on a smaller streamer at this point and they didn't seem interested in the least, so I moved the canoe into a piece of dead water to the side so I could stay put and scanned my fly box.

I didn't want to tie on something that was going to exclude smallmouth from the possibilities, but then again, smallmouth will eat pretty much anything. I'd bet if you tied a deer hair popper that looked like a kitchen sink a smallmouth would crush it as a matter of principle alone. So I picked out this little stonefly nymph buggy looking *thing*, and figured why not. If I was a carp I might eat it. I made a short cast to the opposite bank where a slight eddy formed off some roots protruding into the current and let it swing downstream.

I thought I was snagged. I lifted the rod, it bent over hard, shook and vibrated with tension, and the canoe moved out into the current, pulled by something downstream. I had a 15lb leader on, so I didn't mess with the drag. Line pulled off the reel at a slow and steady pace, up ahead a graveyard of dead fall trees stood out of the water weathered and broken, an ominous sight. I knew this was about to end as fast as it started. I pulled back on the rod trying to turn it, trying to do *something*, but it was pointless to say the least. But in a moment like that, you have to at least be able to say you *tried*.

The fish, we'll all assume carp at this point, it never stopped. It never even paused. Which means it never even looked back, which means I meant nothing to it in the greater scheme of things. How could it mean so much to me, but me so little to it? Had there been more time for the relationship to grow, I'd have been heartbroken. It headed straight into the blow downs, and the line stopped. I pulled, nothing gained, but nothing pulled back either. I pulled some more. I couldn't feel anything on the other end and I pictured the leader in my head, wrapped around a branch the size of my leg, the carp simply sitting down there, reclined in a Lazy Boy reading a magazine without a care in the world, like nothing was going on.

I grasped the fly line with my left hand, pointed the rod tip straight into the water where the line disappeared into branches and darkness, and pulled hard. The leader broke. I sat down, the canoe stopped there in the slow current against the dead and drowned trees. I opened my fly box and tied on another small streamer, one I hoped would grab the attention of a smallmouth...not a carp.

The Judge's Camp

Like most people's childhood memories, a great amount of mine involve my Grandparents. While I spent a lot of time with both sets, my Grandfather on my Father's side is where I dig back to my earliest fishing memories. *Digging* being used mostly as a figure of speech though, as I really don't have to try and remember them. They stay readily available, like a DVD loaded into the player ready to be watched with the touch of a button. And just like a DVD, no matter how many times I replay them, they never wear out.

Most of my stories of fishing with my Father's father usually take place on a small private reservoir on a family farm down in Cobleskill. I can recall so many trips in his truck. The smell of gear oil and diesel strong in the truck cab. The piles of tools, parts, nuts and bolts, cigarette lighters, parts receipts, pocket knives, and various other *things* that covered his dash from one end to the other. The sheets that covered the bench seat, his attempt to keep the oil and grease that clung to the mechanics pants and shirts he wore 24 hours a day from soaking into the seats fabric. Polka music and static found on the AM radio stations. The drives to the farm and back seem just as fresh today as the fishing itself. But the farm trips aren't the earliest I have with him. Before the farm, there was the judge's camp.

Where ever it was, I couldn't tell you, but I don't believe it was far. These were the earliest years, most likely the test years. How far could he take his grandson, and how long could he keep his interest before rocks splashed down and fish retreated, before it was time to go back home, the young boys interest in fishing lost to boredom. Only I don't remember ever being bored, or ever asking when it was time to go home. I'm sure I must have, but I just don't remember it. What I do remember is almost everything else about the place. We'd park next to the camp house, climb a couple steps, open a screen door, and visit with "the Judge" for a while. I'd get handed a soda or some kind of treat while the two old friends visited, and before long, we'd be back outside, walking away from the truck with fishing poles in hand.

We'd stop at a fence next to a barn, and on the other side of the fence was a muddy little stream, and this is the spot that we'd sometimes stop with a coffee can and dig up some worms. We'd move on to the pond, but before the fishing began many times my Grandfather would set down the tackle box and fishing rod, remove a brown paper bag from his pocket, and pick mushrooms under some pine trees. I'd point to some and ask "How about this one?" to which the answer seemed always "No, not that one." They all looked the same to me.

And then there was the dock. It was probably pretty short, but looking back it seemed like a big dock at the time. The pond as I remember it was a good sized pond too, although that also may be inflated by the memory coming from the mind of a small child, to which everything in the world seemed enormous and overwhelming at such a young age. Ahh, the dock. We'd sit on the end of the dock, and watch bobbers float. Grandpa would cast and let it set there for what seemed all day, while I'd cast, watch impatiently, then reel it in to make sure the worm was still there and cast it out to a better spot. A better spot might be way *over there*, or it might be two feet to the left of where it just was. And then there was the goat.

I can still hear the solid clop of hooves on wood and feel each step resonate through the seat of my pants as the goat would sometimes walk, and sometimes trot. Up behind us it would approach, and I hear the gruff laugh of my Grandfather as he'd place a forearm across my chest too. Next came the feel of the goats head pressing into my back. That damn goat was always trying to push me off the dock. I thought it was funny, my Grandfather's laugh probably helped to make me feel more comfortable about the whole situation. But in reality, had I ever been head butted off the dock, I probably would have been traumatized. I didn't learn to swim until the fourth grade.

At some point Grandpa would pick up the tackle box and we'd walk the side of the pond. I'd search for the massive bull frogs that hid in plain sight along the edges, and I can remember the ponds bottom along the outside being lined with chain link fence. I can only assume today that it was there to keep muskrats from eroding away the ponds edge with their destructive tunneling. The path we walked eventually left the pond in the back corner and led through the woods to a creek with some type of manmade dam or something. Grandpa would cast directly into the white water rushing over and hook trout after trout. Sometimes he'd rig two hooks on his line and land two trout, laughing that gruff laugh the whole time.

   Here's the thing about the memories of *the judge's camp*. Thinking back, I don't remember the drives there and back like when I think about the Cobleskill farm trips, and I don't remember what we caught in the pond. But I do remember him pointing out the kingfishers that would swoop down from the trees on the far side of it. The creek outback I know held trout of some kind, only because I remember I couldn't ever catch them...But Grandpa always could. It's just the place and the experience as a whole that I can recall, with such great detail, except for the fish in the pond. I have no recollection of the fish in the pond. This can only support the idea that the fish are the excuse, and that it's something beyond them we're searching for...

The Beginning of the End

I think the last time I fished with Jerry was on the Oswegatchie River, many miles and a couple hours north of here. The whole day is a blur at this point but I know we were there because I was the company welder and one of our guys had taken a portable band saw to a gate and cut the posts off at the ground because the back hoe was too wide to fit through it. Typical.

This was a brand new fence and gate mind you on a cell tower site that wasn't even finished yet when it was cut off at the ground. I imagine when Dave, the back hoe operator, tried to drive in that he was in the frame of mind most of us were always in on those jobs. No surprise that something wasn't done right, and no regrets as he walked to the back of his truck for the generator and the saw, a cigarette between his lips and an air of no cares given. Just another day dealing with someone else's mistakes, just another trip for a couple more guys to fix something else. Not my monkeys, not my circus. But of course it did give Jerry and I a job which in turn afforded us some time on an Adirondack river, so there wasn't much complaining on our part.

I know at that point I wasn't fly fishing consistently yet. I was still carrying a couple spinning rods and only one fly rod that I didn't take out of its tube much yet, and that on the Oswegatchie that day after we welded the gate posts back together and piled the gravel back around the bottom like nothing ever happened we caught quite a few smallmouths just below where the river flowed out of Cranberry Lake.

There was a dam and a walking bridge that we parked by and my favorite, lots of boulders to jump to and plenty of pocket water. We were both fishing spinning rods, we both caught a bunch of fish, and yes, while I was out wading the river and hitting all the pocket water I could and Jerry was playing it safe from the banks...I fell in.

Sometimes when I remember a fishing story I feel like I'm forgetting something if I don't remember falling in I do it so often. I used to blame it on the towers, being a climber and all, thinking I was more sure footed because of it and trying to go anywhere I wanted, but I still stumble and get wet from time to time these days. I haven't climbed in over two years, so apparently I'm just clumsy and take too many chances. But fishing is all about chance anyway so I mean to ring all I can out of each time out, every chance there is I push until it either works out in my favor or not. It's usually a good story anyhow.

JP told me recently as we hiked out from a stream up north that he was going to start hiking and wading like me. I laughed and asked him what the hell he was talking about, what he meant. He said that I just went where I wanted to, I didn't think about it, I never stopped. I just took the next step and hoped for the best. I guess he's probably right. You can't get there if you stand around looking for an easier way all the time.

Now that I think about it, the Oswegatchie River wasn't the last place we fished together. The actual last place was later that night. The hotel we'd found to stay at up there was on a golf course. There were two ponds on the course right behind the hotel and we checked in at dusk. As soon as it was dark we ran a stealth mission out the back door and over a wooden fence to crouch by the ponds and cast into the pitch black.

The reflections of the stars and the moon gave us the only evidence of where the water was it was so pitch black out there, and after about a half hour on each one, we decided that we should've gotten a better look at them before the light was completely gone because there was no evidence of fish life at all. Or frogs, or bugs. They were probably chemically treated golf course ponds, with the way the lawns were trimmed perfectly up to the edges and the fact that there wasn't so much as a weed poking out of the surface anywhere, not a cattail, nothing. But who could blame us for trying?

I haven't worked with Jerry in at least three years, but we've kept in touch as much as social media allows, more than with some family I suppose. It's funny how this world works. Jerry, like a couple of the other guys I used to climb with, picked up the fly fishing bug. A couple of them blame me, but hey, I could've led them in worse directions. I could have steered them into hard drugs that turned them into undependable, broke liars always looking for their next fix, but, oh…wait. *Damn*. Well, at least as long as they brush they won't lose all their teeth fly fishing.

196

So a couple of us have been trying to find time to hit some water together. A couple still climb, a few of us don't. So some are still on the road all the time, and the rest of us always have different shifts at different jobs, families, life, stuff to get in the way. But Jerry and I, we finally made it happen.

The air temperature was only 53 degrees and it was still dark in the woods as we walked in, but it wasn't half as cold as I thought it was about to be when we first stepped into the river, shorts and sneakers. No waders. 53 degrees. We'd both probably like to think that was just two guys refusing the idea that we're getting older and proving we could still take it, but in all honesty on my end anyway, it was just me having all these years under my belt and proving nothing more than I still haven't learned anything. But, I didn't even shiver.

Jerry wanted some help sorting out his casting, I had no idea if I could teach him anything, but after watching me cast a couple times and after me watching him and spewing out a couple tips that I hoped I could explain well enough, and *simple enough*, he had a decent loop going every now and then that kept getting better, and then his first fish on the fly rod, an eight inch smallmouth, so we'll call it ten.

I'm no teacher. I'm no guide. I'm not sure that I could be called anything more than competent at best with a fly rod, but when you've got that and good friends, the rest might all be worth nothing more than diddly squat in the end. And speaking of the end, I slipped him a tapered leader and told him where to get more,   and then told him to go grab another fly line and a spare spool for his 6wt. Yep, I may as well have sent him to a meth house... The beginning of the end.

Private Brook Trout Waters

Here we were, me and JP, on a privately owned lake on fifty-thousand acres of privately owned land in the Adirondacks, gliding away from a submerged dock after John gave a swift push off with his foot. I *wasn't* going to fish the lake, not yet anyhow. I was the only one out of the three of us with a rod. It didn't seem right to me that I should be the only one to cast a line here, to give it a shot while John stood on shore and JP rowed me out. But, I *did* have a new fly rod in my hand, one JP had built for me, and they *both* swore up and down that it was fine. They wanted to know if it was worth the short hike back here after breakfast in another hour as much as I did, so I reluctantly sat on the front of the flat bottom boat, the water swirling to our sides, paddles pushing us across a pitch black nothing below.

The weeds had stopped abruptly about thirty feet from the dock and now there was no bottom, no features, no colors. Just *black*. Staring down into the water was like looking up at the night sky if all the stars and the moon were snuffed out like candles. If it wasn't for the reflections of the trees and the mountain and the blue sky on the surface of the lake, smooth as glass on this end, it would've looked like nothing more than the absence of light. A black hole on the earth.

The night before John had caught a nice brookie out on the lake back at the cabin. The daylight gone, it was in that moment before pitch black but after the sun was completely gone, when we could make out each other's silhouettes and the whites of teeth during a laugh, and the reflection of the moon as a flash on the fly rods length, but not much else. The fish seemed like it was a good size simply by the splashing at the side of the boat and JP said it was a good one as he removed the fly from its mouth, but beyond that all the details were lost. I'm sure it was a great fish as brook trout go, but not being able to make out the white trim of the fins, the orange belly, the blue halos around red spots, the grandness of a good fish is mostly lost when the details aren't seen. We didn't have a light.

That day we'd eaten a dinner the likes of which you'd find in a high end restaurant and then after John's brookie after dark we'd come in and stayed up late around the table playing poker and sipping whiskey and rye, breaking chops and telling stories. It was an odd but comfortable setting to me, the cabin in the middle of nowhere, leaning on the log railing of the porch looking out at the lake, but I wasn't used to the three course dinners and the beds and the card games.

I've read about trips like this but mine normally consist of a pup tent and sleeping bag, a pack of hot dogs and a box of granola bars. I'm not saying I couldn't get used to this type of thing, although I'm afraid that in the end it would soften me up too much and I'd start sneering at offers to fish local streams and camp in tents during black fly season.

Anyways when we woke up on this morning the wind was coming out of the south and after rowing all the way across the choppy lake and back without a fish...ok *JP rowed* and John and I *rode,* we decided the lake wasn't much good for the day in its current condition. The great thing about a private club on fifty-thousand acres in the Adirondacks is that you don't have to work very hard to find another lake to try. You just look to the well beaten trail at the back of the cabin with the nice sign on the tree that points to the next lake and you look at your buddies and when everyone shrugs their shoulders in the *sure why not* body language, you start walking. It's actually too easy.

The idea was to make the sixth tenths of a mile hike to Deer Lake, check it out quick, and be back in time for breakfast. If it looked any good, we'd go back after eating and see how the day panned out. JP grabbed his camera, John a sweatshirt, and I of course grabbed a fly rod. The sign could've pointed to an active volcano, but I wasn't going anywhere without a fly rod. I might do stupid things, but I'm no fool.

So here I was, standing in the front of the boat, JP giving me crap telling me I should learn how to cast so I don't need to stand, John giving me crap from the shore, something about if I caught another good fish I wasn't going to wake up in the morning, all in good fun of course, and I had a glass 7ft 3wt in my hand with a tiny streamer. It was a 5 piece pack rod meant for small streams so why not break it in on the lake? I usually pride myself on being unconventional anyhow. The way I see it, even if you're unconventional and don't do things like they're normally done, if you do them for long enough sooner or later it's bound to work.

OK, maybe I am a fool, but it made as much sense as JP fishing one up in Labrador for monster brookies and catching a pike on the damn thing, so if he could do it, I could catch a little brookie on a lake with a short small stream rod. If there's one thing I've come to believe, it's just fish, just cast, you can't catch a fish if the line's not on the water, so I did.

The streamer wasn't more than an inch and a half long. It wasn't weighted. The line was a floating line. It was bright orange and a stark contrast to the black abyss it shot out across and laid on, looking like a neon sign in a dark bar window. The water could've been ten feet deep or it could've been a hundred. The bottom, most likely a mix of rotting and decomposing rich, black plant matter and black soil absorbed any and all sun light that dared to try and penetrate the lake.

The streamer slapped down like a tiny steak. I stripped line for about fifteen seconds, it was all the time the brook trout could stand to wait. The three weight doubled over, the attack was at the surface and violent, the fishes body twisting and thrashing and splashing. I heard John say something on the shore about "you gotta be kidding me" but I was too absorbed in the fight to get it all.

I held the brookie, easily as long as my forearm with my fingers stretched out and a little past my elbow and we took in the colors. The contrast of the white of the underneath of its jaw and the black of the top of its head. The marbling pattern running the length of its back and the bright blue halos surrounding even brighter red dots, and white trimmed fins looking as pure as a fresh snow fall.

The fish slid from my hand and glided off into the black depth below the boat. I was grinning. JP was grinning, then JP said something I'll never forget. "I can't believe you just caught another good fish just now. You *are* kind of a dick."

Why?

The angler stands at the tailgate, gear laid out as if it were the table containing the sterile surgery tools of a doctor in an operating room. He methodically scans the contents of the fly box before tucking it into the chest pack, one last time going over the patterns, the nymphs, the dries, knowing in his mind that he's got the full ability to match whatever hatch he could find. He inspects the spools of tippet and reassures himself that yes, he does in fact have the necessary strengths and sizes for any situation he may come across.

He assembles his fly rod. His first rod came from a big box store, a cheaper rod and reel combo that got his addiction moving forward, but this rod, this rod came after a couple seasons on the water, and a bonus at work for the long hours put in to hammer out a special project. This rod he had built specifically for him, and as he strings the line through the guides he feels the excitement of what is yet to come, and of the stories it's given him in the past. He hangs his net on his back, pulls his hat down onto his head, and heads off down the trail.

The Trout waits at the bottom of a seam, the water foams with oxygen from the meeting of a slow water to the left and the water crashing down over a deadfall lying across the small river overhead. This is the Trout's hide, its place of comfort. It has no language, it knows no words for what this spot is, it just knows that this is where it needs to be. Here it's hidden from the shapes and shadows that pass above, and it's also here that food is washed downstream and churned up off the bottom below.

It's been a hard life up to this point. In the beginning it was chased out of places such as this by the larger fish, being left to find cover where it could, in places without such an optimal mixture of cover and readily available food. But the fish has lasted past the lives of many lesser trout. It's grown bigger than others, bigger than its surviving brothers and sisters, and bigger than the younger fish who've shown up jockeying for positions that someday might give them the size and

201

presence of this great fish. It sees just ahead of it a tiny black body with protruding legs and antenna, wriggling as it's pushed down stream towards the trout. The brown adjusts its position to its left, and without much of a glance, opens its mouth and eats the meal, moves back to the right, and once again rests, its eyes searching in front and sometimes above.

The angler makes his way down the trail, thoughts of a tight line, a bent rod, and a screaming drag hurrying his pace. A tree branch reaches out and grabs the rod tip, and now he scolds himself for his lack of focus almost leading to a broken six-hundred dollar fly rod. He wonders to himself what he'd do had he snapped the tip off so close to the stream, having no spare rod in the truck even. He quickly comes to the conclusion, he'd press on. Fish with five less inches of rod. There would really be no other option. *Not* fishing isn't ever even a thought. How to continue always blocks out why you couldn't.

Nymphs are beginning to lift off the bottom, squirming and jerking, pushing themselves from their old skins as they prepare to become something entirely different at the surface, and the large trout has taken notice. The trout is particular of which meals it chooses, for no other reason than *it is*. Its fish radar locks in on a specific size, and just barely at the surface, and if these criterions are met, it rises to the occasion.

It has no names for these meals that match the names of the fakes in the anglers fly box. The names were invented by men, instinct is what the trout relies on instead of a vocabulary. It sees, it chooses from something planted deep inside its brain and its being thousands of years ago, and it acts. Its instincts have carried it well to this size and age. It's a wise and old trout as animals with brains the size of plump green peas go. It gets into its natural rhythm of rising and eating at the surface just below the deadfall in the swirls of the tiny plunge pool it calls home.

The angler stands and studies the water. He can see its various currents as if reading a book. He picks out the most likely places, in front of and behind the large boulders, along the far bank just below the leaning willow tree where the leaves of the drooping branches caress the water, the cutout bank, and the deadfall just downstream.

The trunk of the deadfall attempts to block the current but *just* fails, the water spilling over its length and plunging a few inches into a small mixture of water and oxygen. He sees here and there a flutter of tiny brown wings, a caddis hatch is under way, and he can see a large shape rising and eating just below the horizontal tree trunk in the sheltered pool. He does his best to match the color and size, choosing carefully from his fly box.

He takes great care in his knot. He moves into the best position he can put himself in where he knows he can manage the drift of a weightless tiny dry fly as if it were any other real bug without a leader and fly line holding it back, and he's fairly sure the fish could never see him from his place just downstream on the bank. He kneels in the ferns and makes his cast. The perfect cast. The fly lands only inches below the tree trunk and washes into the water of the pool just as any of the other caddis have. It couldn't look any more natural if it were the real thing.

The great brown trout is in a rhythm of rising and resting, it watches from its place below. It sees Its next victim. As the bug floats and approaches, the trout rises and opens its mouth. Just as it's about to take it, its turns back for the bottom and ignores it. It doesn't know why and doesn't question it, it simply waits for the next bug and is pleased to take it. It has no reasoning, nor has it any consideration for the decision it's just made. It's moved on with its life before the anglers fly is even out of sight. The angler is not so lucky. It's a question that will haunt him for the rest of his life... Why?

Made in the USA
Columbia, SC
13 June 2018